ISEB

Independent Schools
Examinations Board

RELIGIOUS STUDIES FOR TODAY

A Textbook for Common Entrance and Common Scholarship Religious Studies

SECOND EDITION

Harry Matthews

© Independent Schools Examinations Board 2004

© Independent Schools Examinations Board
First Edition 2000
Second Edition 2004

Jordan House, Christchurch Road, New Milton BH25 6QJ

All rights reserved. No part of this publication may be sold, reproduced, stored in a retrieval system, or transmitted, in any form or by any means, electronic, mechanical, photocopying, recording or otherwise, without the prior permission of the Independent Schools Examinations Board.

ISBN 0 903627 08 6

Illustrations by Annie Vallotton from the Good News Bible
© American Bible Society, 1976, 1992, used with permission

Printed in Great Britain
by Stephen Austin and Sons Limited, Hertford

CONTENTS

Preface v

OLD TESTAMENT TEXTS

Introduction: Old Testament Passages 3

            The Creation Stories 4

1. The P Creation Story: The Creation 5

2. The J Creation Story: The Nature of Man and the Fall 27

3. Cain and Abel 38

4. The Near Sacrifice of Isaac 46

5. The Ten Commandments 54

6. David and Jonathan 65

7. David and Bathsheba and Nathan's Parable 72

8. Solomon's Wisdom 78

9. Elijah Stories 86

10. The Prophet Amos 95

NEW TESTAMENT TEXTS

Introduction: Jesus in History 107

1. The Temptations of Jesus 112

2. Jesus and the Outcasts 118

3. On being a Follower of Jesus 131

4. Miracles of Healing 145

5. Who was Jesus? 159

6. Parables 169

7. Jesus' Teaching 189

8. The Sentence, Crucifixion and Burial 197

9. The Resurrection 208

10. The Early Christians 216

SAMPLE QUESTIONS for Section 3 of the Common Entrance Syllabus

Old Testament Texts 229

New Testament Texts 235

PREFACE

The aims of this book are to:

(i) provide a commentary upon the set Biblical texts for Sections 1 and 2 of the Common Entrance syllabus, together with a number of practice questions for each topic in Section 3

(ii) explore some contemporary issues which arise from these texts; this has been done at some length for the chapter on Creation

(iii) offer a range of stimulating work from the syllabus for a wide ability range of pupils; in the Contemporary Issues sections there is much overlap with PSHE and the questions set invite the use of drama, art, discussion and some of the varied kinds of writing which the Common Entrance English syllabus requires, such as report writing, letters, newspaper articles etc. Each chapter also offers questions of Common Entrance and Common Scholarship standard.

The author hopes that the material in this book will enable teachers and pupils together to explore more readily the issues which surround

- human existence

- the existence of God

- our responsibility towards our planet

- our responsibility towards each other

- the teaching of Jesus

- personal and public morality

Each chapter normally contains the following sections

- summary of the set Biblical text

- commentary on the text

- questions on the commentary

- contemporary issues

- Common Entrance questions

- scholarship questions

Quotations are from the *Good News Bible*. If a quotation from the Bible is better known in another translation, this quotation is put in brackets alongside the *Good News* version. Bible references are given in the following form: *Genesis 1–2 v 4* means Genesis chapter one to chapter two verse four.

OLD TESTAMENT TEXTS

OLD TESTAMENT TEXTS

INTRODUCTION

OLD TESTAMENT PASSAGES

Genesis

Genesis is the name given to the first book in the Bible. The Old Testament is used by both Jews and Christians. The word *Genesis* means *origin* or *beginning*. Like all the books of the Old Testament, it was first written in the Hebrew language.

Think of your school magazine. Even if each article did not have the writer's name beneath it, you could probably tell that the various sections of your school magazine were written by different people. Each writer has his or her own style, his or her own way of writing. Those who have studied the Hebrew language can tell from the different styles of writing that *Genesis* was written by several writers at quite different periods in the history of the Jews. It certainly was not written by one person over a period of months in the way a book would be written today.

These writers of *Genesis* would have found their stories in different ways. The name given to the place where an author finds a story or a piece of writing or information is called a *source*.

Written and oral sources

Some of these sources would be written ones. Other stories, which had never been written down, the authors would have heard. For example, the stories might have been passed down from parent to child or from teacher to pupil by word of mouth. This could have gone on for hundreds of years with well-remembered stories not changing a word in the retelling.

This passing down of stories by word of mouth is called *oral tradition* and every ancient culture had this because so few people could write. Many precious stories were preserved in this way.

The authors of *Genesis* wrote their parts of this book at different times during the thousand years before Jesus lived. Eventually, around 538 BC, the different pieces of writing were put together by editors to make this first book of the Bible which we know today as *Genesis*.

THE CREATION STORIES

There are two creation stories in *Genesis*. Each was written by a different author, one writing nearly five hundred years before the other. Because it is impossible to find out their names, these two authors are called J and P.

J wrote around 1000 BC. He is called J because whenever he wrote the word for *God*, he used a different Hebrew word from the one used by other writers. When his word for God is put into English letters, it becomes JAHWEH (translated *Lord*). Hence the J.

P wrote his creation story around 500 BC. He is called P because his writings show that he thought that the work of the Jewish priests during his time was very important. He wrote at a difficult time for the Jews. They had been defeated by the Babylonians and he and they had been taken off as captives to Babylon.

J and P would also have heard the religious stories of other cultures, particularly those of Babylon and Canaan. It is not surprising, then, that some of the stories in *Genesis* are very similar to stories found in Babylon. But, as we shall see, J and P were very anxious to show that God was very different from the gods of Babylon and Canaan.

P wrote the first creation story, *Genesis 1–2 v 4a*, which makes it the younger of the two. In this story God created the world in six days then rested on the seventh day, the Sabbath. In the order of creation, man was created last.

J wrote his story 500 years before P. In this story, *Genesis 2 vv 4b–25*, God created the world in just one day. Man was created first and then God created a garden full of plants and trees for the man to cultivate.

THE P CREATION STORY: THE CREATION
GENESIS 1–2 v 25

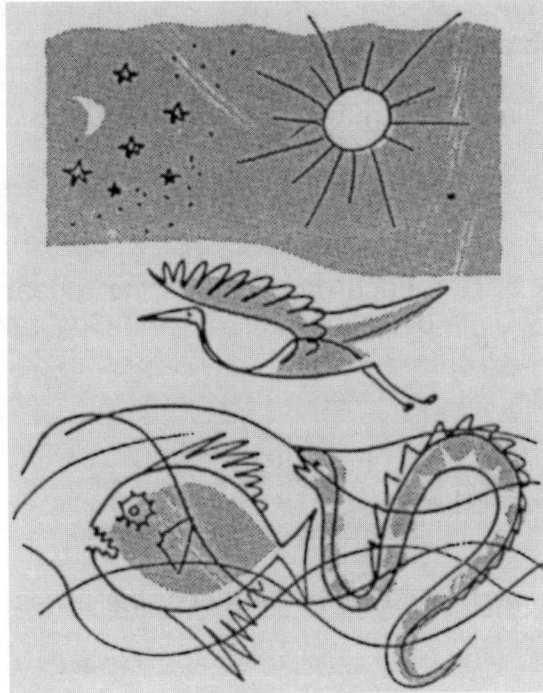

Lights in the sky . . . to rule over the day and the night (Genesis 1 vv 17–18)
Creatures that live in the water and all kinds of birds (Genesis 1 v 21)

SUMMARY OF THE TEXT

The story opens with a description of the Earth which, in the beginning, had no shape.

There was only a raging ocean and total darkness.

The story then gives the details of what God did over the next seven days.

He created by the power of His words alone.

He began each of the days of creation with the command 'Let there be'.

The order of creation:

- the first day: light, night and day

- the second day: the sky or heavens

- the third day: Earth, sea and plants

- the fourth day: Sun, Moon and stars

- the fifth day: fish and birds

- the sixth day: animals and man

- the seventh day: set apart and blessed as a day of rest

After describing the work of God each day, there is the repeated verse: *and God was pleased with what he saw,* or, in other translations: *and God saw that it was good.*

COMMENTARY ON THE TEXT

Genesis 1 v 2 . . . *the spirit of God was moving over the water.*

Another translation of the Bible uses the word *spirit* instead of power. Both these words are a suitable translation of the original Hebrew word. This word is used elsewhere in the Bible to describe a mother eagle teaching her young to fly.

> *The young eagle is in its nest. It is ready to fly for the very first time. It does not know it can fly yet but its mother knows the right moment has come. So she nudges and prods it out of the nest and pushes it over the edge. Then it can become what it was meant to become.*

So in the same way, this Hebrew word in the creation story, which we translate as *spirit* or *power*, carries with it the sense of God's spirit hovering over the water to 'push' the world to become what it was meant to be.

This creation story is unlike the others of that time. The Babylonian creation story, for example, describes creation happening as a result of a fight between gods and a sea monster goddess called Tiamat. The world is then created from the pieces of the monster's body.

Because P knew the Babylonian story, he made the differences between God's creation and the Babylonian one very clear. In P's creation story:

- there is only one God involved in creation, not many gods

- God does not need a monster's body or anything else to make the world

- He does not need any materials to make the world; He uses words alone

- God does not have to fight or struggle with anything to create the world

God was pleased with what he saw or *God saw that it was good*. This part of a verse is repeated after each day of creation. It means that God made everything perfectly; there was nothing evil in what God made. For example, there was perfect harmony amongst all the creatures. In the beginning there was no killing for food, even by animals of other animals. Both animals and man were vegetarian.

The verse also means that all that God had made was ready and fit for the purpose for which He had made it. It was ready for man to get the best out of God's creation by his careful nurture of the land and his care for the animals and plants.

Genesis 1 vv 29–30 *I have provided all kinds of grain and all kinds of fruit for you to eat; but for all the wild animals and for all the birds, I have provided grass and leafy plants for food.*

It was only when the world was very different that God gave man permission to eat meat. After the flood, God said to Noah:

Genesis 9 vv 2–3 *All the animals, birds and fish will live in fear of you. They are all placed under your power. Now you can eat them as well as green plants. I give them all to you for food.*

The Sabbath

Genesis 2 v 3 *He blessed the seventh day and set it apart as a special day, because by that day he had completed his creation and stopped working.*

The word *Sabbath* comes from the Hebrew verb *to rest*.

The Babylonians had rest days in their calendar when all work stopped. Their calendar was based on the phases of the Moon. When they were slaves in Egypt, the Jews had rest days too.

P was very anxious that the rest day was given over to the worship of God. So for him, the creation of the Sabbath day was the climax of his creation story.

Around 586 BC, when he wrote down this creation story, he and the rest of the Jewish people had been taken captive by the Babylonians and the Temple in Jerusalem had been destroyed. In his view, many of these things had happened because his people had not observed the Sabbath day and kept it holy. This, the fourth of the Ten Commandments, had been written down about one hundred years before P wrote his creation story.

This creation story also shows the way in which Jewish days are still measured: from sunset one day to the sunset of the following day:

Genesis 1 v 5 *Evening passed and morning came. That was the first day.*

The Sabbath day is still kept by Jews all over the world from sunset each Friday evening until Saturday sunset. Strict Jews (known as Orthodox) will not cook or drive or light a fire on the Sabbath. Jesus was criticised for breaking the Sabbath by healing on that day. Those who criticised him viewed healing as unlawful work!

Genesis 1 vv 26–28 *Then God said: 'And now we will make human beings; they will be like us and resemble us. . . . Have many children so that your descendants will live all over the earth and bring it under their control. I am putting you in charge of the fish, the birds and all the wild animals.'*

The 'we' in this verse at first seems odd because the Jews strictly worshipped only one God. It was the other peoples such as the Babylonians, who had many gods. The 'we' here probably comes from the idea of a heavenly court. This was a very old idea in Jewish religious thinking. Long ago they imagined God to be in heaven surrounded by beings of a higher order than man but who were not equal to God.

Genesis 1 v 28 *Have many children . . .*

God expects animals and man to produce lots of offspring, to be fertile. The Canaanites, another neighbouring people, believed in fertility gods which were called the *baals*. They had to be worshipped to be sure that the people, their land and their animals were fertile.

When you think about the difficulty of producing food in the ancient world, it is not surprising that the idea of a fertility god was a popular one! The people believed that without the help of such a god the crops would not grow and their animals would not reproduce.

The baals are often mentioned as rivals to God in Old Testament writings. The Prophets often complained in their Old Testament writing that the people of Israel had left God and had started to worship the baals.

In his creation story, P was anxious to show the Jewish people that they did not need to worship the baals. They had no need for fertility gods. Right from the start, the land, animals and man were created fertile. By means of sexual reproduction, animals and man were told by God to produce many generations.

Those who wrote the Bible were never embarrassed to write about sex. P had no doubt that sexual reproduction was given by God so that His will might be fulfilled, that animals and man should be fertile.

The Jewish and Christian religions do not teach that sex in itself is wrong. However, they do offer definite rules about human sexual behaviour. We shall consider those later in the book.

Questions on the Commentary

1. What does the word *Genesis* mean?

2. In which language was the Old Testament written?

3. What is meant by *oral tradition*?

4. Why are the writers of the creation stories called J and P?

5. Where was P when he wrote his story?

6. What effect did neighbouring countries have on the writers of Genesis?

7. Write down **two** main differences between the P and J creation stories.

8. Write down a repeated phrase from the P creation story.

9. Outline some differences between the P creation story and the creation story which Babylonian children would have heard.

10. Explain in full why P, unlike J, wrote a creation story which lasted seven days.

Be an editor

Like a modern newspaper, each book of the Bible had many sources. At some point one person or group of people were given the authority to decide which stories to include and which should be left out of the finished book. The following exercise will give each of you in turn the experience of being an editor.

You will decide which writing will be included and which will be left out. Remember the editor's decision is final!

Divide into groups of four. For each of the following exercises, take it in turns to be the leader of the group, the editor.

As editor you will:

- chair the discussion about what each member of the group thinks should be in the magazine or leaflet

- try to include in the publication a varied selection of what is offered to you

- decide at the end of the discussion what should be put in and what should be left out

- plan one of the following magazines or leaflets:

  (a) a magazine to provide all the information a new pupil will need in order to fit into school life quickly

  (b) a new magazine to appeal to as many of your age group as possible

  (c) the do's and don'ts of parenting: a leaflet to help parents to deal better with children of your age.

For each of these exercises each member of the group should write down **five** things which he or she believes should be included in the publication. The editor's work outlined above will then begin!

CONTEMPORARY ISSUES

There are many contemporary issues linked to the topic of creation. In the pages which follow, four topics will be covered with questions set on each one.

1. ARE THE CREATION STORIES TRUE?

We use the word *true* in several ways. We forget that there is more than one meaning of this word. Let us explore three meanings of *true*.

(i) We use the word *true* about facts such as:

- At atmospheric pressure, pure water boils at 100 degrees Celsius.

- Julius Caesar conquered Britain in 55 BC.

- The Beatles rose to fame in the 1960s.

- Tom missed this lesson because his guitar lesson was changed.

All these facts are provable by finding suitable evidence. They are true for all of us.

(ii) Sometimes we use the word *true* for things which only some of us find true. Poems offer us this kind of truth.

- He made my spirit soar like an eagle.

- Her eyes shone like the stars in the sky.

- My love is like a red, red rose.

You too may have met someone to whom you felt so instantly attracted that you were moved to write poetry like the lines above. Those words would be true for how *you* felt about that person. Yet they would be completely untrue for how the person sitting next to you felt. (At least you would hope so . . . !)

(iii) There is a third kind of truth which is more like the second example than the first. This is the truth a story or film can offer us. Even if a book or a film is not about something which really happened, we can find truths in it, either truths about the way people are, or truths about ourselves. We sometimes praise a book or a film by saying that it is really 'true to life'.

Everyone has heard of the story of *The Boy who Cried Wolf*. There may never have been such a boy, yet this story in one important sense is true!

1. What is true about this story? Discuss its message.

2. Think of some other stories which carry such truths in them.

Jesus told stories known as *parables*. They carry a truth, usually about what God is like or what God wants us to do. This is probably the best way to think about the creation stories. As in the Jesus parables, the creation stories were written to carry a truth about God.

Do not fall into the trap of thinking that all religion is pointless because science shows that creation did not happen over six days as *Genesis* says it did. That is like saying all art is pointless because we now have cameras.

The creation stories in *Genesis* are best thought of as ancient poems or parables.

Sometimes these stories have been called *myths*. The trouble with that name is that it is too closely linked to the idea of untruths or even lies. Parable or poetry is a better name for them because we are used to taking poems and parables seriously. We expect to find in them a worthwhile message, their own kind of truth.

The truth which the writers of the creation stories wanted to share is this: the world did not just happen by accident; it was created by a loving God who really cared about what He had made; above all, He wanted to have a relationship with man – the most important part of creation – whom He had made in His own image.

Discuss these questions before you write about them.

1. Tom says that each of the following statements is true. What do you think?

    (i)   King Arthur pulled the sword called *Excalibur* out of a rock.

    (ii)   Salt lowers the freezing-point of water.

    (iii) My sister Lucy always teases me.

    (iv)   There is intelligent life elsewhere in the universe.

    (v)   My star sign is Scorpio. I am going to have a bad day.

    (vi)   Two's company, three's a crowd!

    (vii) A clear night sky is awesome.

    What would Tom need to do to convince you about each one?

2. Is the first creation story in *Genesis* true?

3. Richard Pinto, an 11-year-old boy from a school in Essex, wrote the following about myths and legends:

    All myths have been useful in aiding the progress of man. They give him hope and fear of doing wrong. But today man has progressed so much that he has confidence to continue alone, unaided by gods or monsters.

    Do you agree with Richard? Give full reasoning in your answer.

4. Read the following statement made by a shocked Christmas shopper, then answer the questions which follow it:

    And we think we are superior. We laugh at superstitions of the ancient world when they believed that gods battled with monsters. We mock the idea that God created the world in seven days. Yet in the year 1999 I saw fifty people, loaded with Christmas shopping in a department store, waiting to feed their date and time of birth into an astrological computer to have their future told . . .

    (i)   Why might we think we are superior to ancient cultures such as that of the Babylonians?

    (ii)   Why was this Christmas shopper shocked?

    (iii) What did those in the queue believe?

13

(iv) What was odd about using a computer in this way?

(v) Why do you think people still believe in astrology?

(vi) What do you believe about astrology?

5. Make up a creation story of your own which explains some of the things that you observe about the Earth, the sky and the world of nature.

6. The poet William Blake describes the experience of seeing 'a world in a grain of sand' in his poem *Auguries of Innocence*:

> *To see a world in a grain of sand*
> *And a heaven in a wild flower,*
> *Hold infinity in the palm of your hand*
> *And eternity in an hour.*

Write a poem or paragraph about what has filled you with wonder or awe.

7. Use magazines to produce a collage which shows how you feel about the Earth today.

8. Design a poster which shares the truth of the Genesis creation story.

9. Use a variety of sources to prepare a five-minute talk on the Babylonians.

2. SCIENCE AND RELIGION

(i) Biblical scholars in previous centuries had studied the lists of Adam's descendants given in *Genesis* and had calculated that the world was about 5000 years old. From the nineteenth century onwards, scientists attacked their conclusions on two main fronts:

(a) The geologists' and cosmologists' findings

By 1830 rock-strata studies and fossil studies revealed that the Earth was considerably older than 5000 years. In the twentieth century the science of cosmology (the study of the universe) has enabled the age of the universe to be estimated at between 15 and 20 billion years!

If all recorded time on Earth is shrunk down to one 24-hour day, look how long it took for man to appear!

00:00: Earth is formed

12:00: first life forms appear

18:00: first life appears which we now find as fossils

20:00: the first fishes appear

21:00: the first amphibians appear on land

22:30: dinosaurs die out

23:50: the monkeys come to the ground

23:59 and 30 seconds, a primate stands on two legs

At the last stroke of midnight, man begins to make tools.

(b) Biological discovery through the work of Charles Darwin

In his book *The Origin of the Species*, Darwin suggested that life on Earth did not form over the period of one day or one week. According to Darwin, life on Earth had gradually evolved over many millions of years.

During this time simpler life forms changed to more complex ones through a series of accidental changes from one generation to the next. The changes which had helped an animal obtain its food or be better protected from predators were the ones which were passed on to the next generation. So evolution led to the survival of the fittest in a species.

(ii) Some implications from Darwin's *Theory of Evolution*

Man is not special or separate.

For the nineteenth-century church leaders, the most frightening idea to face was not how long it had really taken for man to be created. Darwin's theory, which meant that man was not created separately and specially, was much worse and struck a much more severe blow to their beliefs.

As with all other life forms, man evolved from lower, simpler forms of life.

Newspaper cartoons at the time showed an ape in the street, begging for money as a brother to humans. The idea that man, ape and fish all came from the same primitive forms of life caused a huge row between science and religion, a row which for some believers still goes on!

There was no need for a designer (God) – life happened by chance.

Darwin did much of his research on the Galapagos Islands. There, he could see evolution happening before his eyes. He watched the gradual changes which took place in the beak of a bird by choosing a bird which bred very quickly. Different beak shapes would appear by accident. The changes in beak shape which improved the birds' chances of getting food enabled those birds to survive. This better beak shape was, therefore, passed down to the next generation of bird.

(iii) **Some views of scientists today**

Richard Dawkins is a Professor of Science at Oxford University. He is a modern disciple of Darwin. He has described religious belief as a virus which needs to be cured from mankind because it clouds scientific truth in exactly the same way as superstitious belief has hindered medical progress throughout history.

The astronomer professors, Hoyle and Wickramsinghe, however, argue the opposite. They believe that life is far too complicated to have happened by chance. They write:

> *The idea that life was put together by random shuffling is as ridiculous and improbable as the idea that a tornado blowing through a junk yard may assemble a Boeing 747. The aircraft had a creator, so has life.*

(iv) **Is a truce possible between *Genesis* and evolution?**

From the nineteenth century onward, scientific findings have appeared to contradict religious belief. The problem has been largely caused by religious believers reading the Bible as though the creation story were a newspaper report of what actually happened. They read these stories as though they were history rather than religious parable or poetry.

Most of the problems disappear if the creation story is read as a parable and the believer agrees that God used evolution to create the world.

However, some Christians do believe that the *Genesis* stories tell exactly how the world was made and regard ideas about evolution as only a theory, not fact. They are called *fundamentalists* or *creationists*.

It is less controversial to view religion and science as two completely separate human activities which answer two different human questions. Science seeks

16

answers to *how* questions and religion explores the *why* questions. Viewed in this way, they need not be in competition.

Sometimes the discoveries of the scientist can make the world seem more wonderful and add to the awe which the believer already feels about God's creation.

1. How did geological findings and Charles Darwin challenge religious belief in the nineteenth century?

2. The nineteenth-century English poet Tennyson wrote that nature was 'red in tooth and claw'.

   (i)   What did he mean by these words?

   (ii) Does this view of nature mean it is impossible to believe in a loving creator?

3. If most of the conflict between religion and science is resolved by reading *Genesis* as poetry, what problems still remain?

4. The biologist Richard Dawkins writes:

   Nature is not cruel, only pitilessly indifferent. This is one of the hardest lessons for us humans to learn. We cannot admit that things might be neither good nor evil, neither cruel nor kind but simply . . . indifferent to all suffering, lacking all purpose.

   Do you agree with him that the created world lacks all purpose? Discuss this statement fully in your answer.

5. Design a poster which shows the history of the Earth reduced to twenty-four hours.

6. Divide into groups of six and debate the following subjects:

   (i)   life on Earth does need a Designer

   (ii) there is life elsewhere in the universe.

7. What evidence is there in the world for the existence of a God?

   Debate this question. Divide into two groups. Elect two speakers for each group. The rest of the group should provide arguments for the speakers to use in the debate.

3. MAN'S RESPONSIBILITY FOR THIS PLANET

Both the creation stories in *Genesis* carry the message that God put man in charge of all living things and their welfare. Many would say at the start of the twenty-first century that man has failed in that responsibility. What do you think?

In the next section you will be invited to do some research about some of the problems facing our planet and some of the solutions offered. After completing your research, you may come to a different conclusion.

(i)   The state of the planet

Divide into groups to prepare school assemblies on the following topics. Each member of the group should research a different aspect of the subject. Where possible use poetry, music, art and drama to make what you offer as varied as you can.

1. The work of the *World Wildlife Fund*

2. The *United Nations* conference on the planet in Rio 1992

3. The aims of *Greenpeace*

4. *The Green Party*

(ii) The state of the population

The rich get richer and the poor get poorer?

The creation story shows that God intended that the Earth would provide enough food for man, for his offspring and for all future generations.

Today, the world economy works in such a way that many of the people who live in the northern hemisphere have more than enough to eat while some of those in the southern hemisphere have barely enough to survive. Over the years the name for these poor areas of the world in the south has changed from *The Third World* to *Underdeveloped Countries* and now to *Developing Countries*.

The reasons for this imbalance between the richer nations of the north and the

18

poorer ones of the south are varied and complex, but they include some of the following factors:

- Many of the really poor countries do not have industries of their own.

- They have nothing to export to bring money back into their country.

- They may depend upon companies from the northern hemisphere to use them to provide cheap labour and cheap raw materials.

- This benefits both sides.

- The low costs enable the owners to make the goods more cheaply at more profit and the poor at least to have employment, even if it is low paid.

It often means, though, that none of the profit is going back into the poor country to improve conditions. This would be very hard to change. If such companies raised prices to us in order to pay the workers more, we would not buy their goods. The company would go out of business, leaving the poor even poorer!

The poorest countries often have massive debts to the World Bank. They find it difficult to pay even the interest on these debts. Large debt repayment again diverts their money away from improving the living conditions of their people.

Some of the very poor are reluctant to use birth control. While children continue to die of disease, there is a pressure to keep on having large families. This is to ensure that enough children in the family will survive to work for their parents and care for them in their old age, but this increases the number of mouths to feed.

Some very poor countries are not politically stable. Frequent changes of government mean that policies to help the poor are not carried through. The leaders put too much money and effort into staying in power – buying weapons, for example, rather than building schools or hospitals. The leaders of some very poor countries are sometimes corrupt. Such rulers put the money the country earns into their own bank accounts and, again, money is not directed towards improving schools, roads, hospitals or creating jobs.

(iii) **Projects to change things for the better**

Television news often shows terrible pictures of the people of poor countries falling victim to famine and natural disasters, such as floods or a series of bad harvests. Sometimes there are large appeals in the media to encourage us to send money to help the hungry.

The cameras then leave the disaster and move on to the next big item of news. Once the cameras have gone, we forget that country's ongoing need to feed its people.

Charities such as *Christian Aid*, *Oxfam* and *Save The Children Fund* have been working to help poor people help themselves when the media spotlight is not on them.

They believe that developing countries should not just rely on our handouts to survive. By teaching poor people how simple technology can improve their farming, these charities help the poor to help themselves.

The charities send in skilled workers to teach good farming practice and encourage local people to build irrigation schemes and pool their labour to form communes. The communes not only produce enough to feed their families but produce enough to take to market to sell.

Some years ago such self-help aims were summed up in a brilliant poster which read:

GIVE A MAN A FISH AND YOU FEED HIM FOR A DAY
TEACH HIM HOW TO FISH AND YOU FEED HIM FOR LIFE

(iv) **The giving is not all one way . . .**

People in the developing world often have much to teach those in the wealthy nations. Jeremy Hawkey spent a gap year in a very poor part of Nepal helping villagers to build loos and flues (lavatories for better sanitation and pipes in their huts to get rid of poisonous fumes from the cooking fire).

Speaking of the villagers' hospitality, he said:

> *Imagine now that you take a walk to your nearest village and knock on any door. You are a complete stranger. What sort of reception would you get? If you do that in Nepal, you will be asked in immediately and invited to stay as long as you want to – for days or weeks – no matter how poor the people are . . . I went out naïvely thinking I was giving to them. Quite the opposite happened. I returned home as the one who was given more than I could have imagined.*

1. 'Charity is not enough for the developing world.' Discuss this statement before writing about it.

2. What did Jeremy Hawkey set out to do? Why was he surprised at the end of his gap year?

3. Plan a class conference with the title: *Earth – a planet out of control?*

    Divide into four groups.

    Each group must research one of the following topics:

    *   the future of the rain forests

    *   animals under threat

    *   the effects of global warming

    *   the needs of the developing world

    Choose a delegate for each group and pool your research to provide a good speech for your delegate at the conference.

    Choose a chairman to lead the conference.

    After listening to all the delegates, discuss the following questions and come to a decision on them:

    *   What happens next?

    *   What are the priorities for the planet?

    Use the ICT facilities of the school to turn the results of your conference into a class publication in which the speeches and your conclusions are written up and circulated to the rest of the school.

4. Make a collage or design a poster about the environmental needs of our planet.

5. Research the work of *Christian Aid, Oxfam* or *Save the Children Fund* to prepare a school assembly on the topic of *Self-Help Projects in the Developing World.*

4. GENETIC ENGINEERING – IS MAN TAKING THE PLACE OF GOD?

The changing of a naturally-occurring gene pattern in humans, animals or plants, to improve what otherwise would be produced, is called *genetic engineering*.

In the food industry it can be used to produce animals or fruit and vegetables of a certain size or flavour. It can enable wheat to be resistant to disease, to thrive in difficult conditions and to be more cheaply available for the poor.

Genetic engineering remains, however, a very controversial area of scientific research. A big issue of concern is control. Is it possible to make rules, so that only good comes from it and not harm?

For many, a nightmare scenario involving such research was provided by Aldous Huxley in his novel of 1932 called *Brave New World*. His book tells of a future in which human genes are interfered with before birth in order to produce humans designed in the laboratory. Such humans are graded and produced according to the sort of work for which they are needed, from the super-intelligent *Alphas*, who do all the thinking and no manual work, down to the *Deltas* and *Epsilons* who have hardly any intelligence but who are physically very strong. Here is an extract from the book.

> *Alpha children wear grey. They work much harder than we do because they are so frightfully clever. I'm glad that I am a Beta, because I don't work so hard. And then we are so much better than Gammas and Deltas. Gammas are stupid, they all wear green, and Delta children wear khaki. Oh no, I don't want to play with Delta children. And Epsilons are still worse. They're too stupid to be able to . . .*

Such designer babies do not yet exist. However, at the time of writing this book, the Genome Project is well underway. The aim of this research is to make a complete gene map of a human being. Such a map might lead to finding out which genes go wrong to cause some cancers and other diseases, as well as handicaps.

However, even if in one country laws are made to control genetic research, other countries might not want such laws. Some nations might even want to be able to design better humans and use this research on genes to start designing animals and children to have the abilities, skills and features which they want. Imagine what perfect soldiers an aggressive nation might design in order to go to war . . .

1. Discuss the advantages and disadvantages of living in Huxley's *Brave New World*.

2. Should genetic engineering be allowed to continue? How would you decide whether such research is right or wrong?

3. Research is now taking place in genetic engineering. Make a list of **five** rules which such scientists should keep to, in whichever country they are working.

4. If you could produce 'designer' humans, what sort would you produce?

5. Prepare a school assembly on genetic engineering in the food industry. Divide into groups to look at different aspects of this subject.

5.   EUTHANASIA

This word comes from two Greek words which put together mean *easy death*. Today it means giving a drug to help a very sick person to die quickly rather than slowly. Euthanasia is illegal in the United Kingdom.

Some people, while still in good health, decide that if they become very ill, with no chance of recovery, they would like to be helped to die in this way rather than to be kept alive by modern medical techniques.

Euthanasia is performed by administering a large dose of a sleeping drug so that the sick patient does not wake up. Death comes quickly and painlessly by this method.

What seems a straightforward idea, however, has many problems.

Since the time of Hippocratus, a doctor in ancient Greece, doctors have followed his rule that they will use their skill only to help rather than harm a patient. Therefore, many doctors would be unhappy to be put in a position of actually using their skill to kill a patient.

In law, a doctor or anyone else who deliberately causes the death of another person, can be charged with murder despite acting with the patient's permission. For euthanasia to be legal, the law would have to change.

Some families might be very eager to practise euthanasia on an unconscious relative because they want to gain their inheritance.

It occasionally happens that a very ill person recovers and any decision to end this person's life would clearly have been wrong.

Religious people believe that the time of our death is in God's hands, not ours, and it is His will and not our will that should be done.

Divide into groups of five to discuss the issue of euthanasia. If you decide in favour of it, you must produce a set of guidelines in order to prevent its abuse.

Common Entrance Questions

1. (a) In the first creation story, *Genesis chapter 1*, how many days did God take to make the world? (1)

   (b) What did God create on the first day? (2)

   (c) What is created to rule over

   (i) the day

   (ii) the night? (2)

   (d) The creation of man and woman is differently described in the two creation stories of *Genesis*. List these differences. (5)

   (e) Explain as fully as you can why you think that there are **two** creation stories. (5)

   (f) We are told that man has been given responsibility to look after the world which God created. Explain fully whether you think man has done a good job of being in charge of what God has made. (10)

2. (a) In the first creation story, when does God make dry land? (1)

   (b) What was created on the fifth day in this story? (2)

   (c) Write out **two** phrases which are repeated throughout this story. (2)

   (d) Write out the instructions which God gave to man in this story. (5)

   (e) Explain the importance of the seventh day. (5)

   (f) What lessons can we learn from *Genesis 1* about how we should treat the world today? Give reasons to support your answer. (10)

3. (a) In the first creation story, how did God create? (1)

   (b) In *Genesis 1*, how is the Earth described before the first day of creation? (2)

   (c) What did God create on the sixth day of creation? (2)

   (d) Describe how God made humans in the **two** creation stories. (5)

   (e) Explain the importance of the instructions given to humans in **one** of the creation stories. (5)

   (f) 'The creation stories in *Genesis* have little value for today's world.' Discuss this view. Give reasons to support your answer. (10)

4. (a) Explain what you understand by the word *Sabbath*. (5)

(b) Explain why you think that this day was included as part of the creation story in *Genesis*. (10)

(c) Is Sunday trading wrong? Give full reasoning for both sides of the argument. (10)

Scholarship Questions

1. In your opinion, does the world provide any evidence that it was created? (20)

2. 'There is only one purpose on Earth for all living things and and that is to pass on genes.' Discuss this statement. (20)

3. On what basis should genetic engineering be controlled? (20)

4. *The rich man in his castle,*
   The poor man at his gate,
   God made them high and lowly
   And ordered their estate. (19th-century hymn)

   Is it part of God's plan that the northern hemisphere should be much wealthier than the southern hemisphere? (20)

5. In what sense is the creation story in *Genesis* true? Does it offer anything useful today? (20)

6. Outline the arguments for and against euthanasia. (20)

7. Has science once and for all killed off religion? (20)

8. The biologist Richard Dawkins has called religion a *virus*. What do you think he means? Do you agree? (20)

2

THE J CREATION STORY: THE NATURE OF MAN AND THE FALL

GENESIS 3

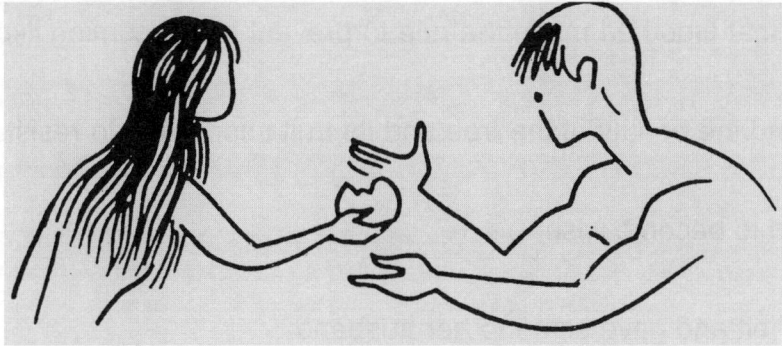

How wonderful it would be to become wise (Genesis 3 v 6)

SUMMARY OF THE TEXT

The Lord took soil from the ground and formed man from it.

He breathed into the man's nostrils so that the man came alive.

The Lord then created a garden in the East called Eden, full of beautiful plants and trees.

Two trees stood in the middle of this garden: the tree of life and the tree which gave knowledge of good and evil.

The Lord God then placed a man in the garden to cultivate it.

The man was told he could eat from any tree except the tree of the knowledge of good and evil.

God then formed the animals and birds from the soil and brought them to the man to see what the man would name them; but they were not suitable companions for man.

While the man was asleep, the Lord God removed one of his ribs and formed a woman from it.

The man and woman were not concerned that they were naked.

The snake, who was the most cunning animal made by the Lord God, then questioned the woman about the rule which God had made concerning what she could not eat.

The snake assured the woman that she would not die if she ate from the tree.

The snake said that God had made the rule to prevent her becoming like God.

The woman found the beauty of the tree and its fruit impossible to resist.

She also wanted to become wise.

So she ate the fruit and gave some to her husband.

As soon as they ate it, they were self-conscious and embarrassed because they were naked.

That evening they heard the Lord God walking in the garden, so they hid from Him.

When they gave the excuse that they were naked, He realised that they had eaten the forbidden fruit.

The Lord God gave the following punishments:

- The snake was doomed to crawl, to eat dust and to be a natural enemy of mankind.

- The woman was doomed to have pain in childbirth and yet still desire her husband whom she had to obey.

- The man would now have to endure hard labour all his life to produce food from more difficult ground.

- Man would die and return to the soil from which he came.

Adam named his wife Eve.

The Lord God then made clothes from animal skins for them.

So that they would not eat from the tree of life, the Lord God banished them from the garden.

COMMENTARY ON THE TEXT

Genesis 2 v 7 *Then the Lord God took some soil from the ground and formed a man out of it; he breathed life-giving breath into his nostrils and the man began to live.*

Hebrew puns

In the Hebrew language, which J used to write this story, there is a pun on the words *man* and *ground*. In Hebrew the word for man is *Adam*. The word for ground is *adamah*.

So the name given to the first man simply means *man!* There is also in the pun the idea that man has to work the soil in order to live and eventually he will be buried in it and become part of it again. There is a very solemn reminder of this in the ritual of some funerals, when earth is dropped on top of the coffin by the mourners round the graveside as these words are said:

>   *earth to earth, ashes to ashes, dust to dust*

God the potter

The idea of the Lord forming man out of soil or clay reminds us of a potter working and shaping the clay to create something. Man is God's work of art.

In the ancient world, breath, like blood, was the sign of life. To make his clay man live, the Lord had to breathe the breath of life into his nostrils.

Genesis 2 v 8 *The Lord God planted a garden in Eden in the East, . . .*

God the gardener

In this story God seemed at times like another human being. He planted a garden, shaped clay like a potter and later on took an evening stroll in the cool of the day!

The word for making other beings human is *anthropomorphism* from the Greek *anthropos* (man) *and morphos* (shape). The cartoon characters Tom and Jerry are anthropomorphic because the cat and mouse speak and react like humans. Usually in science fiction stories, aliens are anthropomorphic (it is much cheaper perhaps!). Christians believe that God actually became a man in the form of Jesus to show man what He was like. God becoming a man is the ultimate in anthropomorphism!

The word *Eden* means *delight*. The East was always linked to a place where wisdom was to be found.

29

Genesis 2 v 15 *Then the Lord God placed the man in the Garden of Eden to cultivate it and guard it. He said to him, 'You may eat of the fruit of any tree in the garden, except the tree that gives knowledge of what is good and what is bad.'*

Adam was put in the wonderful garden to look after it. There is no idea here of idle luxury; Adam had to tend the garden. The Lord, like a landlord, paid occasional visits after Adam's day's work to see that His garden was being looked after.

In Adam, however, the Lord had not made a robot. Adam was given free will. He was able to make choices for himself. When the Lord gave Adam the rule about the tree of knowledge, He also gave him the freedom to disobey that rule. That is how the Lord made man.

The knowledge of what is good and what is bad here means knowing about everything that there is to know. It is not just about knowing what is right and wrong.

Genesis 2 v 18 *Then the Lord God said, 'It is not good for the man to live alone.'*

God again used soil to create the animals and birds which were brought to man for naming. In the ancient world, to know someone's name was to have power over them. This is what was clearly intended here. Allowing man to name creatures meant that he was to have authority over them. However, animals would not be enough of a companion for man. Finally, with Adam's own rib, God created a woman as a suitable partner. Adam's poem of joy, 'Bone taken from my bone, flesh from my flesh . . .' means that Adam felt that they were partners and equals! Eve started off inside him, so they are one. *Verse 24* carries this idea on to a thought about marriage. When two people are married, they become one again. It is a very deep union. In the wedding service couples are reminded of this when they are told that marriage makes them of 'one flesh'.

Genesis 2 v 25 *The man and woman were both naked, but they were not embarrassed.*

J highlighted the childlike innocence of Adam and Eve before they had eaten from the tree of knowledge. Little children can run about naked unselfconsciously and that is what Adam and Eve were like. For the society in which J wrote, adult nakedness was a source of shame. This was not so in the Canaanite cultures where the gods, the baals, presented a constant temptation to the Jews. It was important, therefore, for the Jewish people to have strict views about nakedness to preserve what was different about them.

Genesis 3 v 1 *Now the snake was the most cunning animal that the Lord God had made.*

J was not in any way suggesting that the snake was the devil. He was anxious not to shift the blame to the snake for what was to follow. The writer wanted to make it clear that it was the woman and the man who had to take responsibility for their decision to disobey God. The story also suggests that even before they gave in to the temptation to eat the fruit, there was, in both the man and the woman, the desire to be like those in God's court or God himself. That desire or curiosity seems to be part of the way man is made.

Genesis 3 v 7 *As soon as they had eaten it, they were given understanding and realised that they were naked; . . .*

Nakedness was considered highly improper in ancient Israel. The Israelites were anxious to be completely different from the Canaanites who followed the fertility gods called the *baals*. So the eating of the fruit had not made the woman and the man like gods in their new knowledge. They had gained nothing, only shame. By their act, they had lost paradise: Eden. They were also to lose that ease of meeting with God as He strolled in the garden to meet them there for the last time. Afterwards, when they heard him coming, they could feel only shame and guilt, two totally new emotions.

Their sin (wrongdoing) serves to divide the man and the woman rather than to unite them. The man blamed the woman. The woman blamed the snake. The punishments served to answer the questions which ancient people would have asked about snakes, the pain of childbirth, the rule of man over woman and the hard work necessary to survive from the land.

Genesis 3 vv 20–21 *Adam named his wife Eve . . . And the Lord God made clothes out of animal skins for Adam and his wife . . .*

In Hebrew the word Adam means *mankind* and the word Eve means *Mother of all living*. In the face of what had happened, Adam's choice of name for the woman was a great act of faith that, in the face of hardship and death, the woman would continue to produce life.

That God made clothes for Adam and Eve shows that he wanted to help, preserve and show His care for them. In spite of all, they would continue to matter to Him and be deeply loved by Him.

So Adam and Eve had to leave the garden for ever, in case they ate from the Tree of Life. The way back to Eden was placed under a double guard so that it was impossible to return. They now had to face a life of hardship in order to survive. Yet that life would be one in which they would remain cared for by the God who had made them in His own image and who would not abandon them, even though they had disobeyed Him.

Questions on the Commentary

1. What is the link between the word *Adam* and *ground*?

2. What did *breath* mean to the ancient world?

3. Which word describes turning other creatures into human beings?

4. What does the Hebrew word *Eden* mean?

5. What is the significance of man naming the animals?

6. Which part of this creation story is taken into the marriage service?

7. What significance does this have for marriage?

8. Why is nakedness a recurring theme in this story?

9. Why does the writer of this story avoid linking the snake with the devil?

10. What evidence is there that Adam and Eve were divided rather than united after they had eaten the forbidden fruit?

11. What were the punishments for the snake, the woman and the man?

12. What did Adam do to show that he had faith in the future?

13. What did God do to show that He still cared for Adam and Eve?

CONTEMPORARY ISSUES

This story is known as *the Fall of Man*. In the story, mankind fell from the perfect garden – a paradise – down to our world of pain, hunger, hard work, suffering and death. The cause of this fall was man's disobedience.

Like the *Creation* story, the *Fall* story is a parable. But what is its message? Was it written simply to explain to the ancient world why snakes crawl rather than walk, why women have pain in childbirth and why all things return to the ground when they die?

Or does this parable have something to tell us about human nature, whichever century we live in?

1. ARE WE BIASED TOWARDS THE BAD RATHER THAN THE GOOD?

(i) There is an independent boarding school in Suffolk called Summerhill. Children do not have to go to lessons if they do not want to. An important part of this school's life is the School Council in which every child has a voice and a vote. All the rules of the school are made by the School Council. All members of the school, children included, have an equal voice at these meetings. Meetings are called regularly to discipline children and to make and change school rules. At these meetings both teachers and children can express strong feelings and have the freedom to use any swearword if they want to.

At a meeting to decide whether bedtimes should be abolished, the headmistress made the point that the last time there was no rule about bedtimes everyone suffered.

1. In groups of six, decide what you think are the three most important rules in your school. Also find out from the group which rules they find are the most difficult to keep.

2. Why do schools usually discourage swearing? Why do you think it is allowed at Summerhill?

3. Why do you think at Summerhill everyone suffered when bedtimes were abolished?

4. Imagine that you are standing as a candidate for your School Council. Write a short speech to try to persuade people to vote for you.

5. Design a poster to advertise what is good about your school.

(ii) About seven children are murdered by strangers each year. The number has not varied for many years. While every murder is a tragedy, it is soon followed by a further one.

News of a murdered child causes parents everywhere to clamp down on any small freedoms they have dared to give to their children: going to the shops on their own, or going for a walk, or camping with friends in the garden.

33

Every tragic death of a child adds one more piece to the awful picture of the world which the media give us day after day: all strangers are evil; it is not safe to go out alone; murder and robbery waits around every corner; the world is an evil place.

Sadly, much more harm is done to children by people they know than is ever done by strangers. Wrapping our children up in cotton wool to protect them from the bogey men created by the media is robbing them of their independence.

The frightening world which television chooses to show in order to guarantee good viewing figures is, alas, the one we believe in.

1. What does the writer mean by the *further* tragedy which follows the murder of a child?

2. Do you believe that your neighbourhood is safe enough for you to be given more independence?

3. Why does the writer believe that television news is about bad news rather than good?

4. What effect does the writer think that this has on our view of the world?

5. Provide some evidence that the world is a better place than the one shown in the newspapers or on television.

2. **THE VALUE OF A HUMAN BEING**

When they meet, Hindus bow to each other. They are bowing to the spirit of God which they believe is in every person. Christians and Jews believe that God made man in his own image. Therefore, the creation story teaches that every human life is unique, valued and special.

A fifteen-year-old girl wrote the following about herself.

Finish the piece of writing with your thoughts about what makes you unique and especially you!

> I am me.
> There will not ever be anyone like me.
> I am stardust and dreams.
> I am light.
> I am love and hope.
> I am hugs and sometimes tears.
> I am . . .
> I am . . .
> I am . . .

Common Entrance Questions

1. (a) From which forbidden tree did Adam and Eve eat in the Garden of Eden? (1)

    (b) How did Adam respond to God's call, 'Where are you?'? (2)

    (c) Which **two** punishments did God give to the serpent? (2)

    (d) Describe what happened when God sent Adam and Eve out of Eden. (5)

    (e) Explain what this story teaches about God. (5)

    (f) What are the similarities between Adam and Eve and the people of today? Give your reasons carefully. (10)

2. (a) What was the name given to the garden in which Adam and Eve lived? (1)

    (b) What did the serpent promise Eve? (2)

    (c) What did Adam and Eve do immediately after eating the fruit? (2)

    (d) Describe the punishments which were given to Adam and Eve. (5)

    (e) Explain why you think Adam and Eve acted in the way they did in this story. (5)

    (f) 'This story still has a very important message for today's world.' Do you agree? Give your reasons. (10)

3. (a) Which rule did God give to Adam and Eve? (1)

    (b) What was the name of the garden in which they lived? (2)

    (c) Which piece of knowledge was Eve tempted to gain? (2)

    (d) Describe what happened to Adam and Eve when they gave in to temptation. (5)

    (e) Which punishments were given to Adam and Eve? (5)

    (f) Why do you think this story is called the 'Fall of mankind'? Give full reasons. (10)

4. (a) In the Garden of Eden what were Adam and Eve forbidden to do? (1)

    (b) Who tempted Eve? (2)

(c)   Why did Eve give in to the temptation?   (2)

(d)   Describe what happened to Adam and Eve when they gave in to the temptation.   (5)

(e)   Explain why you think the punishment for Adam and Eve was so severe.   (5)

(f)   What advice would you give to someone who finds it difficult to resist temptation today? How might they benefit from that advice?   (10)

Scholarship Questions

1.   (a)   *'And the Lord God made clothes out of animal skins for Adam and his wife, and he clothed them all.'*

        Describe the events leading up to this action by God. Does anything surprise you about this verse?   (8)

   (b)   Do you think that mankind is still 'fallen'?   (12)

2.   (a)   If God made Adam and Eve perfectly, why do you think that they were vulnerable to temptation?   (8)

   (b)   If you and your classmates had to spend a year on a desert island without adults,

       (i)   how would you choose a leader

       (ii)   what would be your most important rules

       (iii)   what do you think would be the biggest threat to your survival?   (12)

3.   If you had the chance to create a world like ours, what changes would you make in its design to improve it? Your answer can include changes to human design.   (20)

4.   (a)   Describe the punishments which were given to the snake, Eve and Adam after they had eaten the fruit from the Tree of Knowledge.   (8)

   (b)   Do you think that punishment is a successful way of changing human behaviour?   (12)

3

CAIN AND ABEL

GENESIS 4 vv 1–16

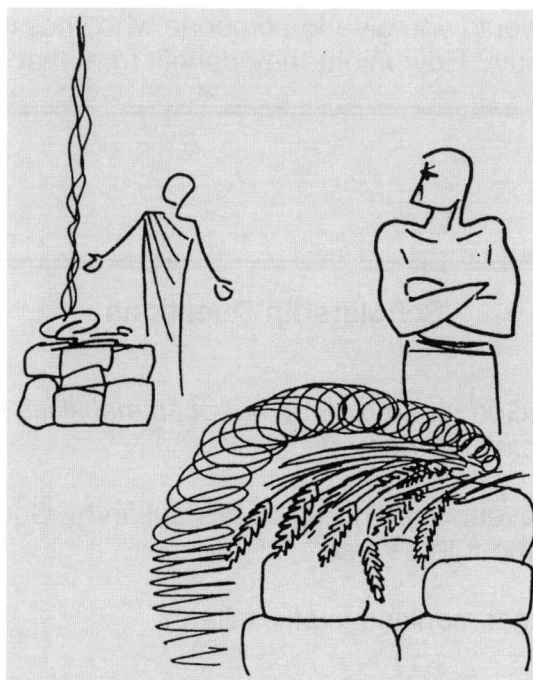

Why that scowl on your face? (Genesis 4 v 6)

SUMMARY OF THE TEXT

This story shows that once man has rebelled against God, he is capable of doing any kind of evil to his fellow man.

Cain and Abel, the sons of Adam and Eve, brought offerings of thanks to God.

God accepted Abel's lamb but rejected the portion of Cain's crop.

Cain was furious and, despite God's warning about where such anger might lead, he took his brother out into a field and killed him.

As a punishment, Cain was cast away by God from his homeland to fend for himself.

COMMENTARY ON THE TEXT

Clearly the differences between Cain and Abel ran deep. They were divided as brothers, not only in the work that they did, but by Cain's attitude to Abel. This came to the surface when Abel's offering to thank God for his lambs was accepted and Cain's offering was not.

There is no explanation given in the story as to why Cain's offering was not considered good enough by God. This is meant to show that God's reasons must be a mystery to man. Man must accept God's decisions, whether they seem fair or not. Life is like that. Once man starts to question God, then things go wrong.

vv 6–7 *Then the Lord said to Cain, 'Why are you angry? Why that scowl on your face? . . . sin is crouching at your door. It wants to rule you, but you must overcome it.'*

So, even though Cain's offering had been rejected, God was still very much concerned about his welfare. God pointed to the temptation to do evil which He knew was lurking in Cain's heart.

Cain took no notice of God's concern and so the first murder took place. In the Fall story, God appeared to Adam and Eve immediately after the wrongdoing. In that story He asked the whereabouts of Adam and Eve. Here again He appeared immediately after the crime and asked Cain where Abel was. Cain answered: *I don't know. Am I supposed to take care of my brother?* (King James' version of the Bible: *. . . am I my brother's keeper?*)

Cain's reply, as translated in the King James' version of the Bible, has become a saying: *I am not my brother's keeper.* This means: do not ask me about him (or her!). He has a life of his own, his welfare is not my responsibility. Don't blame me if anything happens to him, or because something bad has happened to him!

God asked the question because He thought the very opposite was true. God believes that we all do have a responsibility to be our brothers' (and sisters'!) 'keepers'. He has created us in order that we look after each other's wellbeing. That is the standard from which Cain had now so dreadfully fallen by his act of murder.

v 10 *Your brother's blood is crying out to me from the ground . . .*

The Jews believed that there were two ways in which a man could die: by loss of breath or by loss of blood. Both breath and blood belonged to God. Therefore, Abel's blood, his life which belonged to God, was crying out to God from the ground. It could not simply be hidden and the evidence buried as Cain had tried to do. This adds to the drama. The blood of the murder does not just belong to the victim; it was God's property, which is why God turned up at the scene of the crime so soon!

Cain's punishment

There are many similarities between Cain's punishment and the style of punishment given to Adam and Eve.

- Part of Adam's punishment was that the soil would not be as fertile, so he would have to work much harder in order for it to produce the food needed to survive. So too with Cain.

  v 12 If you try to grow crops, the soil will not produce anything; you will be a homeless wanderer on the earth.

- Also, just as Adam was cast out of Eden, Cain was to be sent away.

- God showed care for Cain in the punishment and protected him. (Remember how God made clothes for Adam and Eve as he was sending them out of the Garden of Eden.)

  v 15 So the Lord put a mark on Cain to warn anyone who met him not to kill him.

So, again, in the face of man's failure, God was not prepared to give up. No matter what man did, even after punishing him, God continued to care about him. God protected and supported his future.

Questions on the Commentary

1. What is the message of this story?

2. What does *I am not my brother's keeper!* mean when used in daily life?

3. Why were Cain's attempts to hide Abel's blood doomed to fail?

4. What similarities are there between Cain's punishment and that which was given to Adam?

5. Make a list of families you have come across in the Bible in which jealousy is a destructive force.

CONTEMPORARY ISSUES

This is the story of the first murder. It takes place between brothers. Statistics today reveal that murder is, sadly, all too common amongst family members.

Families are units in which extremes of feeling are regularly aroused. Every emotion, from deepest love to deepest hate, and all levels between, are regularly produced in family relationships.

Jealousy is a powerful and damaging force in all relationships. It is especially destructive within a family.

1.   YOU HAVE ALWAYS LOVED HIM MORE THAN ME

Sarah was three when David was born. Until then she had been the apple of everyone's eye. Her parents worked hard at not making her feel left out when all the attention was on the new baby. They made sure she received presents too. When David was a baby, Sarah was never unkind to him and she was happy to be with him and to care for him. But as she got older, whenever she was in trouble she was very quick to say to her parents, 'It's always the same. He gets away with murder and I get an earful for the slightest thing. You have always loved him more than you love me!'

1.   If you were Sarah's parents, how would you reply to Sarah's last statement?

2.   If Sarah confided her feelings of jealousy to you as a friend, what advice would you give to her?

3.   Write about a time when you felt jealous and describe how you coped with it.

4.   Describe the perfect family.

2.   AM I MY BROTHER'S KEEPER?

(i)   *One night in the mid 1950s two teenage boys found themselves trapped by a policeman on a factory roof. They had been trying to rob the factory when the alarm had gone off and brought the police to the scene of their crime. The older boy, Derek Bentley, 19, was in the custody of a policeman on the roof when the younger boy, Christopher Craig, 16, shot another policeman dead. Although Bentley did not fire the gun or possess a gun and was mentally retarded, he was executed for the crime of murder. Craig, at 16, was too young to face the death penalty and was sent to prison.*

> 1.   In one version of what happened on that roof, Bentley is said to have shouted to his friend Craig, 'Let him 'ave it Chris!' What two interpretations are there to this instruction?

> 2.   Imagine that you are a headmaster in the 1950s at the time of this trial. Write an assembly talk after the judge has passed sentence on the young men.

(ii)   *A group of four school friends were playing together at lunch break. Three of them were ten and the fourth, Robert, was nine. They began a fun 'bundle' in which, like puppies, they were soon rolling round the ground, all arms and legs everywhere. It was hard to say why it happened, but suddenly Robert began to cry. Yet the bundling continued. Gradually he began to realise that one of the boys was hitting him for real while the rest just stood and watched.*

Robert was still white and shaken when his mother picked him up from school at four o'clock. She knew something was wrong. He told her that he had been bullied by four boys.

> 1.   Do you think that what Robert said to his mother was accurate?

> 2.   Why do you think that the others just watched Robert being continually hit by someone a whole year older?

> 3.   You are one of the ten year olds who ended up watching what was going on. Write this story again from your point of view.

> 4.   Write this incident as a script which could be acted out as a class / school assembly. Let the drama be about what happened and what should have happened.

(iii) *During the Second World War, to set an example for all the prisoners in a concentration camp, the commanding officer chose six of the prisoners to go and dig a grave. He said that the grave would be for one of them whom he would choose when they had completed the task. When the hole was dug, the Commandant stepped forward and pointed to a young man whom the guards pushed to one end of the hole ready to be shot.*

One of the five remaining grave diggers happened to be a Catholic priest.

'No, take me instead,' he insisted. 'He has a young wife and two small children who will need him when the war is over.' The guards took him at his word and shot the priest instead.

1. Divide into groups of eight and re-enact this story.

2. Rewrite this event from the point of view of either:

    a guard

    the young man who was saved

    the priest.

3. Research the topic 'twentieth century martyrs' for an assembly talk. Include in your talk information about Father Kolbe (commemorated in Canterbury Cathedral).

Common Entrance Questions

1. (a) Who was the elder son, Cain or Abel? (1)

   (b) How did Cain and Abel earn their living? (2)

   (c) What were the different offerings which the two brothers brought to the Lord? (2)

   (d) Explain why Cain became angry and what sin he committed as a result. (5)

   (e) Explain what you think is the purpose of this story. (5)

   (f) What do we mean today when we say that 'the punishment should fit the crime'? Give examples to support your answer. (10)

2. (a) What was the name of Adam and Eve's first born son? (1)

   (b) What work did Cain and Abel do? (2)

   (c) Which offerings did Abel and Cain bring to the Lord? (2)

   (d) Describe how Cain became angry and the sin he committed as a result. (5)

   (e) Explain why you think God accepted one offering and not the other. (5)

   (f) Cain was punished for what he did. Is it right that we should always be punished for breaking rules and laws? Give examples to support your view. (10)

3. (a) Describe the first murder as told in the Old Testament. (5)

   (b) Describe the punishment which God gave. (5)

   (c) Have you found that punishment changes people's behaviour for the better? Explain fully. (10)

Scholarship Questions

1. *Am I supposed to take care of my brother?* or *Am I my brother's keeper?*

   What does the Bible tell us about our responsibilities towards each other?   (20)

2. The Bible seldom provides a story of happy families – the first one begins with a murder! Why do you think this is the case and what is there for us to learn from these stories?   (20)

3. 'Life is not fair!' Cain would have said that. Do you agree with him? Provide full reasons for your answer.   (20)

4

THE NEAR SACRIFICE OF ISAAC

GENESIS 22 vv 1–19

Now I know that you honour and obey God (Genesis 22 v 12)

SUMMARY OF THE TEXT

God tested Abraham by asking him to sacrifice his long-awaited and much-loved son Isaac.

Abraham followed God's instructions and took Isaac to a mountain in the land of Moriah.

Once on the mountain, Abraham carefully prepared for what Isaac thought would be an animal sacrifice.

However, Abraham obeyed God and tied up his son.

He was about to kill Isaac when an angel of God told him to stop.

The angel told Abraham to offer instead a ram which was caught up in a thicket.

Because Abraham passed this test, God promised him that he would have as many descendants as there were stars in the sky or grains of sand on the seashore.

These descendants would be able to conquer their enemies and all nations would seek God's blessing because of Abraham's obedience.

COMMENTARY ON THE TEXT

Abraham had waited so long for Isaac who had been a gift from God to him and Sarah in their old age. So Abraham's test of faith was particularly hard!

Isaac was also Abraham's only link with any future descendants he might have. The act of killing Isaac would seem, then, to go against what God had already promised Abraham *(Genesis 12)*, that he would be the father of a great nation. That Abraham was prepared to go along with God's wishes is an enormous proof of Abraham's complete faith and trust in God's purpose for him and his son. There is no evidence anywhere else in the Bible that the Jewish people sacrificed children. However, it is possible that the people of the local Canaanite culture did sacrifice children to their gods, the baals.

There are many kinds of sacrifices mentioned in the Old Testament. Sacrifices are offerings to God. They are usually the best of the crop or the best animal (as in the Cain and Abel story). The word sacrifice carries with it a sense of costly giving.

In Jewish religious ceremonies, animals would be sacrificed as a sign of thanks, as in the Noah story when the flood subsided *(Genesis 8 v 20)*. The Jewish people followed very full directions about when and what to sacrifice.

The whole of the first seven chapters of the Old Testament Book of *Leviticus* deals with these instructions. In chapter sixteen of that book there is also the idea of the *scapegoat*, an animal on which all the sins of the people are placed.

Leviticus 16 vv 21–22 Then the goat is to be driven off into the desert by a man appointed to do it. The goat will carry all their sins away with him into some uninhabited land.

The word *scapegoat* has passed into our language. It is used of someone who takes the blame for what others have done.

Questions on the Commentary

1. Why was Abraham's test a particularly harsh one?

2. Which neighbouring culture went in for child sacrifice?

3. Where do Jews find instructions about sacrifice?

4. Where does the word *scapegoat* come from, and how is it used today?

CONTEMPORARY ISSUES

1. SACRIFICE AND RELIGION

The need for man to offer sacrifices is as old as religion. Whenever man has believed in a god, he has felt the need to please that god by offering animals, crops or even fellow humans as a sacrifice.

For Christians and Jews, the idea of sacrifice is still a very important one. They would regard sacrifice as a way of showing that God is first, not second or third. This, of course, was the point of Abraham's test too.

To put God first was very much at the centre of Jesus' teaching. Jesus saw that the test which God had given him went beyond even what Abraham had had to do. Jesus believed that it was God's will that he had to offer his own life as a sacrifice. Like Abraham, he was completely obedient to God's will.

Christians believe that Jesus' death on the cross was a sacrifice for the sins of the world, rather like the scapegoat. Jesus' death is linked, therefore, in Christian belief, to God's forgiveness. When, today, Christians break bread together and share it, the broken bread reminds them of Jesus' sacrifice for their sins. They also believe that when they break bread in this way, Jesus is with them.

48

1. Why are religion and sacrifice so closely linked?

2. What are the parallels between Jesus and Abraham?

3. When are Christians particularly reminded of Jesus' sacrifice?

4. Use the library to prepare a talk on Lent.

5. Design a poster against selfishness.

2. SACRIFICE OUTSIDE RELIGION

Painting by numbers

Emily didn't often return to Liverpool now that all her family had long since died. She had come for a conference and couldn't resist driving very slowly along the streets of her childhood.

She could still remember the exact numbers of the houses to which she had delivered papers: 4, 7, 11, 18, 22, 24, 26, 31 and so on. She was amazed how easily they all came back thirty years later. It was all for ten shillings a week (50p), through rain, snow, fog and dogs. She not only delivered them seven days a week but collected the money for them, too, on Saturday afternoons, before the evening delivery.

The best part was the Christmas tips. Over £5 most years. Imagine, ten weeks' wages given to you on one glorious afternoon of collecting.

Then she remembered the year of her favourite Aunt B's depression and how, in a moment of utter reckless abandon, Emily spent all her Christmas tips not on what she had been saving for but on a giant 'Painting by Numbers'. As soon as she saw it in the shop, she knew that working on that was just what her aunt needed to cheer her up.

That Christmas Emily had nothing for herself from her own money but at least she knew her aunt was enjoying working on the painting.

The following November Aunt B took her own life. As Emily parked outside where Aunt B used to live, she remembered the happy times, her laughter, her welcome, her cakes and, most of all, her pleasure in painting by numbers . . .

1. What does the passage tell you about Emily as a person?

2. Explain how what Emily did was a sacrifice.

3. Describe an occasion on which you gave something away in a moment of 'utter reckless abandon'.

4. Finish this story:

> I was feeling really peckish when I remembered the Rolos in my pocket. There was just one left. I was just about to eat it when in walked . . .

3. OBEDIENCE

John Friars was delighted to open his vicarage door to see his friend Father Bill Lyons, the local Roman Catholic priest, standing on the step.

'I've just come to say cheerio, John – I'm off. The bishop rang last night and he wants me to be in Birmingham on Monday to start again in a new parish.'

John Friars stood there for a moment, open-mouthed.

'Bill. Come in! What news! What about the job scheme, your half-finished youth club centre, your . . . ?'

The list of things which Father Bill had started and was involved in was endless. He was a great success and now, because of a phone call from his bishop, he was off. Just like that. Lock, stock and barrel. That weekend, Bill Lyons would disappear from his wonderful work that he loved in the East End of London. As sure as his faith, he would start again on Monday morning as a wonderful parish priest one hundred miles away.

That's what I call obedience, thought John Friars. He wondered how he would feel if his 'phone were to ring now with the same marching orders . . .

1. Why would Father Bill find moving difficult?

2. How did he seem to be reacting to what he had been told to do?

3. Write about a time when you found it difficult to obey.

4. Research a talk on the vows of poverty, chastity and obedience.

5. Imagine that when you go home this evening, you are told that you are moving to the USA next month. Describe your feelings on hearing this news and write fully about what you would miss.

4. FAITH IN WHAT . . . ?

It is said that we live in a materialistic age. This means that many people believe that happiness and fulfilment lie in having expensive things.

Materialism is the belief that, given plenty of money, the right job, car, clothes and the right neighbourhood to live in, we will be happy and fulfilled. That is the faith of our time.

River Phoenix was a successful young film star. By the age of twenty-three, when he died, he was rich and famous. This was written about his death:

This screen idol was supposed to be vehemently anti-drug, pro-environment and supposedly a clean-living film star who wouldn't so much as look at a diet coke. Yet he died on the sidewalk on 31 October 1993 at 8825 Sunset Boulevard, apparently of a self-administered drug overdose.

1. What do you understand by the words *materialistic age*?

2. From magazines, produce a collage with the title 'Materialism, Today's God'.

3. Imagine that you are a famous film star at sixteen. Write a page of your personal diary in which you express your hopes and fears and problems.

4. Do you think that it is inevitable that film stars who are successful in their early teens will end up like River Phoenix?

Common Entrance Questions

1. (a) Where did God tell Abraham to take his son Isaac?   (1)

    (b) Why was Abraham taking Isaac on the journey?   (2)

    (c) What question did Isaac ask his father on the journey?   (2)

    (d) Describe what happened when Abraham and Isaac reached their
         destination.   (5)

    (e) Explain what this story tells us about religious faith.   (5)

    (f) This event was a test for Abraham. In which ways do you think people
         might find their faith being tested today?   (10)

2. (a) Where was the mountain on which Abraham was told to sacrifice
         Isaac?   (1)

    (b) After the donkey had been left behind, who carried the wood for the
         sacrifice?   (2)

    (c) What did Isaac say to his father on the way up the mountain?   (2)

    (d) What do we learn about Abraham from this story?   (5)

    (e) What do you think of Abraham's actions in this story? Give your
         reasons.   (5)

    (f) We would not, of course, expect this kind of sacrifice to happen today
         but most religions expect their followers to make some sort of
         sacrifices for the sake of their faith. What might these be and why?   (10)

3. (a) Who told Abraham not to sacrifice Isaac?   (1)

    (b) What did Abraham then look around and see?   (2)

    (c) Which name did Abraham give to the mountain afterwards?   (2)

    (d) Which promises did the angel of the Lord give to Abraham?   (5)

    (e) Explain what this story teaches about Abraham.   (5)

    (f) Do you think it was fair of God to test Abraham in this way? Give full
         reasons in your answer.   (10)

Scholarship Questions

1. What parallels are there in the story of Abraham and the story of Jesus? (20)

2. (a)   How was Abraham's faith put to the test? (8)

    (b)   What part does sacrifice play in religion today? (12)

3. Is sacrifice bribery? Use examples from the Bible in your answer. (20)

4. 'Materialism will continue to be the faith of the masses in the twenty-first century.' Write your views in full about this claim. (20)

5

THE TEN COMMANDMENTS

EXODUS 19 vv 1–8, EXODUS 20 vv 1–17

THE IMPORTANT IDEA OF COVENANT

The Old Testament contains a series of covenants between God and the people of Israel. A covenant is a promise made between two parties. Each side has to keep its part of the promise. Another more everyday word for a covenant would be a *deal*.

'If you will give me your Oasis CD, then I will let you have my number seven iron.'

The Bible constantly shows God as trying to maintain a good relationship with a people who seem always ready to worship other gods such as the baals. So God makes a series of offers; a series of *If . . ., then . . .* offers, a series of covenants. The one which began the faith of the Jewish people was the covenant with Abraham.

If Abraham and his people worshipped only God, **then** God would treat them as his people and would be their God right down through the generations.

He promised Abraham that if he accepted this covenant, then Abraham would be the father of a great nation. Abraham agreed and circumcision was given by God as the sign of that covenant. All Jewish boys are still circumcised on the eighth day after birth. Circumcision is an ongoing reminder of that first promise between Abraham and God.

The next important covenant between God and his people was the one with Moses. This took the form of the giving of the Law. God gave Moses these commandments in order to help the people not to sin and thereby damage their relationship with Him.

SUMMARY OF THE TEXT

Before stating what He expected from the people (their side of the deal), God reminded the people of Israel of all He had done for them.

He had brought them out of Egypt where they had been slaves.

The Ten Commandments

    1. *Worship no god but me.*

    2. *Do not make for yourself images to worship.*

    3. *Do not use my name for evil purpose.*

    4. *Keep the Sabbath as a holy day.*

    5. *Respect your father and mother.*

    6. *Do not commit murder.*

    7. *Do not commit adultery.*

    8. *Do not steal.*

    9. *Do not accuse anyone falsely.*

    10. *Do not covet another person's property.*

COMMENTARY ON THE TEXT

The First Commandment

This forbids the worship of gods other than Yahweh. This is a very important commandment. The people of Israel were often tempted to worship other gods. They gave in to the temptation because of their need to keep the land and animals fertile. In Canaan the local fertility gods were mother goddesses. So as a sort of insurance, to try to guarantee good produce, the people would sacrifice to the baals as well as to Yahweh *(see below)*.

The Second Commandment

This forbids the making of images of gods carved out of wood or stone, including making images of Yahweh Himself. By giving examples of the forbidden images, the commandment reminds the people of the gods of the surrounding people.

The sun, moon and heavenly bodies would be the shapes of some Babylonian and Egyptian gods. Egyptian gods were often in human and animal form or combinations of both. *In the waters under earth* were the fish gods of Syria and Philistia and in Egypt the crocodile was holy.

Archaeological excavations of these regions have produced no statues of Yahweh. However, many statues of Canaanite mother goddesses have been found. It is very likely that some Israelites, whilst keeping to the commandment about statues of Yahweh, housed these statues to help along their crops because it was the local custom to do so.

The Third Commandment

We feel upset if we are teased about our name or if someone makes fun of our name. For the Jewish people, names were even more important and to misuse a name was a deep insult against another person. This, of course, would be even more true about the name of God.

At certain periods in their history, the Jewish people felt this so strongly that, in order to protect God's name, they used substitute words. So, instead of writing or saying out loud their word for God, they would use phrases such as *The Most High* or *The Eternal*.

The Fourth Commandment

The background to the Sabbath law is stated fully in the earlier chapter on Creation. The word *Sabbath* is linked to the Hebrew word for *rest*. A calendar based on the phases of the Moon and the seven-day week was developed in Babylonia. For the Jews it was the keeping of the Sabbath, as well as the rite of circumcision, which enabled them to feel bound together as a people and to be different from non-Jews. Non-Jewish people are called *Gentiles*.

After the time of Moses, the Jews were reminded to use the Sabbath day as a day to think of the greatness and the goodness of God when He released His people from slavery in Egypt.

The Fifth Commandment

The importance of this commandment to the people of Israel is shown by its position in the list. Duty towards parents comes immediately after duty towards God. The commandment is not just for children to take notice of, but anyone who has parents. Old and weak parents especially are to be cared for.

This is the first commandment which carries a promise. The promise of long life is for the nation as well as for individual people. It carries the belief that for a nation to be strong, its family life must be stable and strong.

Commandments Six, Seven and Eight

These have been called the *Three Pillars* upon which all societies must rest. These pillars are:

- respect for human life

- marriages must not be broken by unfaithfulness

- the right to have property which should be safe from theft

The taking of life refers to murder. All countries permit their citizens to kill an enemy in war and until the twentieth century most countries would execute criminals who committed certain offences.

The Ninth Commandment

This is about lying in court (perjury) or telling lies about someone else. A reputation for honesty is one of the most valuable attributes which a person can have. To be known as someone who readily lies, damages your relationships in family, school, among friends and in business.

The Tenth Commandment

This is unlike the others because it is not about an actual deed but about an inward feeling. Such feelings, of course, could lead to action if you set about trying to get from your neighbour something you envy.

What is different about the Ten Commandments?

The rules of other cultures were often concerned about what their people should do to worship their god properly: the details of ritual. By contrast, the Ten Commandments are about what the individual must do if he or she wishes to do right actions rather than wrong ones. This is called acting morally.

The commandments were given as a COVENANT which follows the usual 'If . . ., then . . . ' pattern.

If the people of Israel ignored these commandments, **then** God might abandon them.

Questions on the Commentary

1. Which gods from other cultures do the Ten Commandments hint at?

2. How do we know that the Canaanites worshipped mother goddesses?

3. What does *perjury* mean?

4. Why are the Sixth, Seventh and Eighth Commandments called the *Three Pillars*?

5. What is different about the Tenth Commandment?

6. How do these commandments for the people of Israel differ from the rules for other cultures?

CONTEMPORARY ISSUES

1. WHAT IS MORAL?

Morality is concerned with not only **knowing** what is right and wrong but **doing** it. As we all know, knowing is not enough. We have all done bad things, knowing that we were doing wrong.

We call people moral if they have a good reputation and immoral if they have a bad one. Today there is a worry, often expressed in newspapers, that too many people have lost all sense of what is right and wrong and just do as they please.

There are several reasons why this has happened.

(i) Today, fewer people follow a religion than in the past.

Religious people usually have a very clear sense of what is right and wrong. However, that does not mean that they will all agree with each other on all moral issues.

For example, some Christians believe that homosexual relationships are wrong whilst others do not. Some believe that abortion is always wrong, others do not. Yet both sides will believe that they have been guided by God in arriving at what they believe to be the right view.

(ii) **Today there is a view that what is right and wrong depends upon custom or fashion.**

In this view, things are only wrong if the people around you decide that they are. So, if you live in a culture which allows more than one wife, or does not mind you having sexual relations with many partners, or taking drugs, then it is not wrong to do these things. This view is flawed. The Nazi party in Germany believed it was necessary to kill Jewish families. Clearly the fact that thousands of Nazis believed it right to kill Jews did not make the holocaust right.

So some things must always be wrong, wherever you live and no matter what the customs of the local people are.

(iii) **Films and television have had a strong influence on language and behaviour.**

Television series, films and pop videos set fashions not only in clothes but in behaviour and language. For example, some families are less strict about swearing now. So much is heard on television and in films, that the parents are less worried when swearing happens.

The influence of films and television is a bit like the influence of friends on a large scale. In order to fit in with our friends, it is always tempting to copy much of what they do. In a similar way, the life style of film, pop and sports idols is one which is tempting for the young to follow.

There is a continuing debate about whether sexual scenes or violent scenes on film or television affect people's behaviour.

1. Make a list of things that you think would **always** be wrong no matter which country you lived in.

2. Do you think that using bad language matters?

3. How far would you agree that films and television affect people's morals?

4. Do you think that sexual and violent scenes in films and on television are harmful to children's moral development?

2. HOW MORAL ARE YOU?

How do you decide whether to do the right thing or not?

- Are there rules / laws / conventions to follow, e.g. 'If I do that, is it stealing?'

- What are my own guidelines? An example would be:

    Usually I try not to do things which will hurt other people.

    Another well-used guide is The Golden Rule which is:

    Do unto others as you would have them do unto you.

    Many people would say that they use this as a guide for their moral actions.

- What will happen if I get found out? Sometimes we so much want to do what we know to be wrong that all we think about is risk. Perhaps doing the wrong thing is worth it because not much will happen even if we do get found out.

- If everyone else is doing it, it must be all right to do it. This is called *peer-group pressure*. It is the reason why many young people start smoking, drinking, using drugs recreationally or experimenting with sexual relationships.

Test yourself on the following exercise:

For each of the following situations write down:

- what you would do

- why you have made that choice.

1. You come across your brother's personal diary. Do you look through it?

2. You overhear a conversation in which lies are being told about your best friend. Do you interrupt and speak on your friend's behalf?

3. Someone you don't particularly like invites you to an excellent film which you have not seen. Do you go?

4. You find a briefcase containing photographs which would embarrass a well-known person. Do you sell them to a newspaper or give the briefcase back to its owner?

5. Your seventeen-year-old daughter is an actress. She is offered a part in a film in which she must do a nude scene. Do you allow her to accept the part?

6. You have agreed to sell your car to a close friend. A stranger offers you four hundred pounds more. Do you accept this offer?

7. You discover a code which allows you to make free telephone calls anywhere in the world. Do you use it?

8. Your car needs a new clutch. Do you sell it without telling the buyer?

9. Your ten-year-old son has been invited to a sleepover at which a 15 video will be shown. Do you let him go?

10. Your sister is going out with your best friend who you know is seeing someone else. Do you tell her?

- Discuss your answers with the rest of the class.

- Design a poster which advertises The Golden Rule.

3. **ONLY ONE COMMANDMENT NOW . . .**

In his book *Devil's Advocate*, the radio and television news interviewer John Humphrys writes that shopping on Sundays has, to some extent, replaced going to church.

Not only do the shopping centres often ape cathedrals architecturally with their domes and their naves but, in a bizarre way, they now fulfil the role which cathedrals used to fill. Shopping is what we believe in. The whole family visits the shopping mall. We have loyalty cards to make us feel we belong. We queue, as for Communion. There are murals, as in churches. The availability of free credit offers you paradise on Earth. Here is the big difference: there is only one commandment: thou shalt buy.

1. If the writer of this piece were writing from a strictly religious point of view, which of the Ten Commandments might he consider to be broken when people shop like this in a mall on a Sunday?

2. In the writer's view, what has shopping provided in people's lives, apart from the things they buy?

3. Do you agree with what John Humphrys is claiming about the role of Sunday shopping in people's lives? Support your opinion with full reasoning.

Common Entrance Questions

1. (a) When they received the Ten Commandments, which country had the Israelites recently left? (1)

   (b) What did God promise the people of Israel if they kept his covenant? (2)

   (c) What are the first **two** commandments? (2)

   (d) Explain why you think God gave the Ten Commandments to the people of Israel at this point on their journey. (5)

   (e) Which do you think are the **three** most important commandments? Give full reasons in your answer. (5)

   (f) Some schools have written rules, some schools do not. If you were the head of a school, would you have a written set of rules? Give full reasons for your answer. (10)

2. (a) Where did God make the covenant with Moses? (1)

   (b) How did the people react to Moses' meeting with God? (2)

   (c) Write out **two** of the commandments which focus upon the relationship between God and humans. (2)

   (d) Write out the commandments which focus on human society. (5)

   (e) Explain what is meant by *covenant* and why this covenant was so important for the people of Israel. (5)

   (f) How important are these commandments today? Give full reasons for your answer. (10)

3. (a) Which mountain did Moses go up to meet with God? (1)

   (b) God made a covenant with Moses. What is a *covenant*? (2)

   (c) What are the two sections into which the Ten Commandments can be divided? (2)

   (d) Write out the Ten Commandments in your own words. (10)

   (e) What do you think is the reason for having rules? Give examples of rules which you consider to be either helpful or unhelpful. (10)

Scholarship Questions

1. 'Good and Evil do not exist in themselves. They are what people decide.' Write in full your opinion about this claim. (20)

2. 'Television has contributed more than any other factor to the decline of standards in behaviour amongst our young.' Would you agree with this statement? Present your views in full. (20)

3. You are the head of a school. Write the outline suggestions for your staff as to how children could gain a moral education. (20)

6

DAVID AND JONATHAN

1 SAMUEL 20 vv 1–23

SUMMARY OF THE TEXT

As a result of King Saul's jealousy of him, David was on the run.

He secretly approached Saul's son, Jonathan, and asked him why his father wanted to kill him.

Jonathan tried to reassure David, but David insisted that his life was in danger.

David devised a test of Saul's attitude.

He told Jonathan that he would not be turning up at the New Moon Festival meal.

If the king showed anger at David's absence, this would be proof that he intended to harm David.

They then went out into the fields to think of a signal so that Jonathan could let David know how Saul had reacted.

Jonathan made David promise to continue to love him as his closest friend, even through this trouble.

They agreed on a signal.

David was to hide where he had hidden before.

Jonathan would then fire three arrows.

He would send his servant to fetch them.

If he said, 'The arrows are on this side of you,' then David would be safe.

If he said, 'The arrows are on the other side of you,' then David was in danger.

Jonathan finished by saying that the love they had for each other would be forever.

COMMENTARY ON THE TEXT

This story shows how Jonathan proved his loyalty to David by his willingness to discover what his father (King Saul) really felt about David. Jonathan also promised to help David escape his anger.

v 5 Tomorrow is the New Moon Festival . . .

This was a religious festival which not only marked the new moon, but also the first day of the month. Saul clearly intended to have a special meal for this festival at which he would expect David to be present.

v 14 . . . be loyal to me . . .

In the Hebrew, in which this story was written, the word for *loyal* and *love* is the same. Loyal love would be expected in the closest of human relationships, as between David and Jonathan, and also between man and God.

The very close friendship between David and Jonathan represents the closest relationship possible outside a sexual one. When, later in the story, David heard that Jonathan had been killed in battle, he sang a lament which included the words:

> *I grieve for you my brother Jonathan*
> *How dear you were to me!*
> *How wonderful was your love for me,*
> *Better even than the love of women.*

Their friendship has also become a way of describing two inseparable friends. Of such friends it may be said, 'Oh, they are a David and Jonathan, that pair.'

Questions on the Commentary

1. What is the theme of this story?

2. Why did the people of Israel celebrate New Moon?

3. Why did David need Jonathan's help?

4. Explain the signal which Jonathan agreed to send to David.

5. In which way does the passage link loyalty and love?

CONTEMPORARY ISSUES

1.   THE ABSENCE OF FRIENDS

(i) *In the early hours of last Monday morning, Kelly Yeoman killed herself because she could no longer stand the constant bullying by the gang of youths who hung around outside her house . . . Five youths have been arrested (one girl) and are now on police bail. And since then, everyone has been asking why? Why did that family get singled out? Why did the school not pick up on Kelly's problems? Why did she have no friends to help her? The youths called Kelly and her family the Slomans and persecuted them because they were unemployed, belonged to the Salvation Army (Kelly played the tambourine), were overweight and powerless. Apparently the gang feel ashamed of themselves now. But it is too late. Probably the gang did not think of Kelly and her family as people with feelings but simply as objects to be made fun of, whose weakness could make them feel stronger.*

1. If a friend confided in you that she/he was being bullied, what advice would you give her/him? In which ways would you show your loyalty to that friend?

2. Why do you think the gang did what they did?

3. Design an anti-bullying poster for your school.

4. Plan an anti-bullying assembly. Use readings, music and drama to make your point and to provide advice which is in line with the school's anti-bullying policy.

(ii) In his book *Devil's Advocate*, John Humphrys, from BBC News, writes the following about the 'bedroom culture' of young people today which keeps them away from friendships:

. . . one fifth of children aged four and under have their own television in their bedroom. By the time they reach the age of eight the figure rises to one third and by eleven it is two thirds. They spend three hours a day in front of either a television or a computer screen. A 1999 London School of Economics report . . . concluded that more and more children are retreating from the real world into a bedroom culture. The vast majority of parents do not like it – here's the odd thing, neither do the children. They are resentful at not being allowed out and say they find television boring.

1. What do you think John Humphrys means when he claims that 'children are retreating from the real world into a bedroom culture'?

2. Do you agree with the report findings that young people find television boring?

3. Why are young people not allowed out?

4. Write a diary entry for a perfect day.

2. **THE PRESENCE OF FRIENDS**

Sarah writes:

In October my friend Hugo, who had been diagnosed with Aids about two years ago, fell seriously ill. He rapidly went downhill – it was obvious he wasn't going to get better, so we arrived at the hospital to care for him in the last stages of his illness. The night before he died, we sat up with him in his hospital room. It was not like a scene from opera. Instead of wailing family, and friends throwing themselves on the bedclothes in agonies of grief, we sat on the bed, drank several bottles of Campari and watched Hell Raiser 11 on video. Hugo kept us all entertained despite his pain, and the nursing staff let us get on with it – it was quite a party.

. . . I came away from the hospital having found the courage to love someone, having allowed myself to be loved and having shared that experience with others. These are very simple, ordinary and inexpressibly precious things.

1. In which ways could Hugo have caught Aids?

2. What does this extract tell you about the sort of friendship that Sarah and Hugo had?

3. Why do you think loving someone takes courage?

3. **CHOICES**

There are three rooms. You have to spend two hours in one of them. One contains a Play Station with a selection of games you would like. The second contains a television with your favourite channels. The third contains someone of your age whom you have not met before.

Which room would you choose to spend the time in? Explain the reasons for your choice.

Common Entrance Questions

1. (a) Why was David afraid of King Saul? (1)

   (b) Where did David go to hide from Saul? (2)

   (c) What excuses did David ask Jonathan to make on his behalf? (2)

   (d) Describe how Jonathan helped to save David's life. (5)

   (e) Explain, as fully as you can, why Jonathan acted in this way. (5)

   (f) Which qualities do you think make someone a good friend? (10)

2. (a) Where was David supposed to be for the New Moon Festival? (1)

   (b) What was David's excuse for being there? (2)

   (c) What did Jonathan make David agree to? (2)

   (d) Describe what Jonathan suggested to David to let him know whether Saul wanted him dead or not. (5)

   (e) Explain what this story tells us about the character of Jonathan. (5)

   (f) Jonathan lied to his father in this story. Do you think it can ever be right to tell lies? Explain your answer carefully. (10)

3. (a) What was the relationship between Saul and Jonathan? (1)

   (b) Why did David have to flee King Saul? (2)

   (c) What was David's excuse for not being at the banquet? (2)

   (d) Describe how Jonathan helped to save David's life. (5)

   (e) Explain why Jonathan acted in this way. (5)

   (f) Jonathan did everything he could for the sake of David. Write about someone who did everything she/he could for the sake of others and explain why she/he did it (10)

Scholarship Questions

1. (a) Describe the relationship between David and Jonathan and how it was tested. (10)

   (b) Is there such a thing as the perfect friend? Write fully from your own experience. (10)

2. It is possible that Adolf Hitler took encouragement from the result of the Oxford Union debate in the 1930s, when the students voted not to fight for King and Country. What do you think would be the result of such a debate today? Outline the arguments for both sides. (20)

3. A journalist recently wrote the following about how televisions are used instead of people as child minders.

   > *I try to imagine a group of experts in the pre-television age discussing the best way to bring up children. One of them suggests something like this: 'Shut 'em up in their bedrooms for several hours a day with no company except a box in the corner that pumps out moving images . . . Some of the things they watch will be educational; much of it will be rubbish, often coarse and vulgar or even violent and full of crude language and sexual innuendo. You will not be able to monitor what they watch because you will not be with them. But at least they will be occupied and will not be getting up to mischief.'*

   (a) Do you think that too much exposure to television inhibits children's willingness to make friends? (8)

   (b) Give your opinion on the journalist's view of television. (12)

7

DAVID AND BATHSHEBA AND NATHAN'S PARABLE

2 SAMUEL 11 vv 1–17 AND 2 SAMUEL 12 vv 1–9

SUMMARY OF THE TEXT

2 Samuel 11 vv 1–17

One day, when David was king, he went up to the roof of his house from where he could see a woman bathing.

After finding out that she was Bathsheba, the wife of Uriah (one of the officers in his army), he sent for her and made love to her.

Not long afterwards Bathsheba told David that she was pregnant.

David sent for Uriah to come back from the battlefield.

However, when he did come home Uriah refused to sleep at home the first night and on the second night.

Even after David had made him drunk at supper, Uriah still insisted on sleeping away from home.

This was because his men were sleeping in the open still; he felt he should do the same.

The next morning David arranged by a letter to Joab, Uriah's commander, for Uriah to be sent to the front line of battle where the fighting was heaviest.

As David had hoped, Uriah was killed in the next battle and Joab sent a messenger back to David with the news.

After a period of mourning, David took Bathsheba as his wife.

She gave birth to a son but God was not pleased with what David had done.

2 Samuel 12 vv 1–9

The Lord sent the prophet Nathan to visit David.

Nathan told David the following parable.

A rich man and a poor man lived in the same town.

The rich man had many cattle and sheep.

The poor man only had one lamb which he took care of and nurtured tenderly.

One day, a visitor arrived at the rich man's home.

The rich man, instead of killing one of his own animals, killed the poor man's lamb for food for the visitor.

David was angry and said, 'The man who did this ought to die.'

Nathan said to David, 'You are that man.'

COMMENTARY ON THE TEXT

When Bathsheba told David that she was pregnant by him, he first tried to conceal his action by bringing Uriah home and giving him leave from the army. David would have expected him to sleep with his wife immediately so that Uriah would think that the baby was his own. This plan failed because Uriah was so committed to the life of a soldier that he could not bear to sleep in the comfort of home while his comrades continued to suffer the discomforts of sleeping out of doors.

David then arranged for Uriah to be sent to the front line in order for the adultery to remain hidden by Uriah's death in battle. Uriah was an heroic soldier and did not question his fate.

God then sent the prophet Nathan to tell David a parable which was really about what David had done. When David heard the parable, he unwittingly brought judgement upon himself. Nathan went on to tell David what his punishment from God would be:

- As Uriah died by the sword, so in every generation some of David's descendants would suffer violent deaths.

- The child which David had given Bathsheba would die.

This idea that the punishment for your evil deeds goes on to the next generation and beyond is a very old one and often appears in the Old Testament.

Today, when suffering the loss of a loved one, people will still ask, 'What have I done to deserve this?' So the idea that disease and death are punishments is still around.

However, Christians do not believe this. Jesus saw his work as being very much for the outcast and the sinner to bring them back to God's forgiveness, not to suffer His punishment.

The Bible tells it as it is . . .

David is thought of as Israel's greatest king, a model for the expected Messiah. Yet he committed adultery and organised the death of one of his faithful officers. David shows the mix of good and bad which is in all of us. The Bible is by no means full of perfect people; its stories lay bare all their faults as well as their strengths. In short, the Bible shows us what it is like to be truly human.

Questions on the Commentary

1. What was David's first plan when Bathsheba told him she was pregnant?

2. Summarise the evidence in the text which shows that Uriah was a first-rate officer.

3. What task did God give to Nathan?

CONTEMPORARY ISSUES

ADULTERY – MANY COMMANDMENTS ROLLED INTO ONE

(i) During their RS lesson, 8H was asked which of the Ten Commandments they thought was the most serious to break. Jeremy gave the following answer:

I think it's the one about adultery, number seven, 'cos if you think about it, if you commit adultery, you are breaking several others at the same time. You are stealing another person's marriage partner and you have coveted that person's partner before taking him. You are both living lies with your respective partners and it has been known that murder has been committed when an adultery has been discovered. You could even say that the person you are having the affair with has become your idol and taken the place of God. Finally, in committing adultery, you are bringing dishonour to your family and therefore not respecting your parents.

1. How far do you agree with Jeremy's answer?

2. In which ways do you think adultery damages family life?

(ii) In 1999 the President of the United States of America finally admitted that he had had an 'inappropriate relationship' with a young female member of his staff. When first asked about the possibility that such a relationship was taking place, he denied it. When the American people were given opinion polls about the President's eventual confession, over 60% of them said they wanted him to stay in office. They believed that he was good at his job. For them, what he did in his private life should have been kept private and had no bearing on whether or not he was a good president.

1. Do you think it matters if a country's leader is unfaithful to his or her partner?

2. Should he or she be allowed to continue in office? If not, why not? If so, why?

3. Should the news media be allowed to publish details about the private lives of political leaders?

Common Entrance Questions

1. (a) Which prophet paid a visit to David? (1)

    (b) For whose death had David been responsible? (2)

    (c) In the parable which the prophet told, what did the poor man own? (2)

    (d) From the same parable describe what the rich man did and how David reacted to the story. (5)

    (e) Explain why you think a parable was used to show David his guilt. (5)

    (f) What message might the prophet's parable have today? Give reasons for your answer. (10)

2. (a) Where had David sent Joab and the Israelite army? (1)

    (b) Where did David first see Bathsheba? (2)

    (c) Why was Uriah reluctant to leave his troops? (2)

    (d) Describe what happened to Uriah, and how his death was reported back to David. (5)

    (e) Compare the characters of David and Uriah from this story. (5)

    (f) Do you think that national leaders should set a good example in their personal lives? Give reasons to support your answer. (10)

3. (a) Who was Uriah the Hittite? (1)

    (b) Who was Joab? (2)

    (c) When David sent for Uriah, why did he refuse to go home? (2)

    (d) Describe briefly how and why Uriah was killed. (5)

    (e) From these events, compare the character of Uriah with that of David. (5)

    (f) In France newspapers are forbidden by law to publish the details of a politician's private life. Should Britain have the same law? Give full reasons to support your view. (10)

Scholarship Questions

1. Write a character study of King David. (20)

2. (a) Write a brief character study of Uriah the Hittite. (5)

   (b) Retell how Nathan made known God's displeasure to David. (5)

   (c) Why is adultery destructive to family life? (10)

3. Do you think it would matter if a nation's leader were an adulterer? (20)

4. Does our society still need marriage? (20)

8

SOLOMON'S WISDOM

1 KINGS 3

Don't kill the child (1 Kings 3 v 27)

SUMMARY OF THE TEXT

David's son, Solomon, was a young king who, after offering a sacrifice to God at Gibeon, heard the voice of God in a dream.

During the dream, the Lord asked Solomon to choose a gift.

He asked for the gift of wisdom.

Solomon felt that above all else he needed wisdom to rule God's people *with justice and to know the difference between good and evil.*

The Lord was so pleased that Solomon had asked for wisdom, rather than long life or riches or the death of his enemies, that He gave Solomon not only what he asked for but great wealth and honour too.

The Lord also promised that if Solomon kept His laws and commands, he would have long life as well.

Solomon then woke up and made offerings to the Lord.

Two prostitutes came before Solomon with a story.

They both had had babies within two days of each other, but one of them had rolled on her baby and it had died.

In the night she had taken the other baby and claimed it as her own.

Each mother argued in front of Solomon that the baby who remained alive was her own.

Solomon then sent for a sword and ordered the baby to be cut in half.

One of the women cried out for the the swordsman to stop and begged that the baby be given to the other.

However, the other woman said, 'Don't give it to either of us; go ahead, cut it in two'.

Then Solomon knew who the real mother was, so the baby was returned to her.

When the people heard of Solomon's decision, they respected him and knew that God had given him wisdom to settle disputes fairly.

COMMENTARY ON THE TEXT

v 3 Solomon loved the Lord and followed the instructions of his father David, but he also slaughtered animals and offered them as sacrifices on various altars.

Solomon ruled from 970–933 BC and his lasting achievement as king was the building of the Temple in Jerusalem. It was destroyed by the Babylonians in 586 BC. The Temple was the one place to unite the people in the worship of God. Until its completion, altars were set up around the country on the same sites which the local Canaanite people had used for their worship.

v 5 That night the Lord appeared to him in a dream . . .

Often in the Bible a dream is the medium through which God speaks to humans, especially if the person has been praying at a holy place (a sanctuary).

v 9 *So give me the wisdom I need to rule your people . . .*

Solomon's request was for a gift of character to help him be a good king. Some sources suggest that he was only around fourteen when he became king. It is therefore not surprising that he felt that he needed to ask for wisdom in order to be an effective leader at such a young age. His request was a very practical one. Wisdom for him would mean the ability to make good decisions about people and the affairs of state. He would then not rush into things but be able to consider all possibilities and outcomes.

v 15 *Then he went to Jerusalem and stood in front of the Lord's Covenant Box . . .*

David had made Jerusalem the capital. This had the great advantage of helping to unify the tribes and make them focus on one place for the king to rule. Solomon was to achieve the same for religion by building the Temple there. The covenant box was where the commandments of the Lord were kept. It was also known as the *Ark*. It was the holiest place for Jews and was believed to be a place of God's presence.

Today in any synagogue the Books of the Law are kept in a special cupboard called the *Ark*. These books continue to be a sign of the covenant which God made with his people.

A note on Solomon's reign

Solomon, like his father David, went through a ceremony of anointing when he was made king. This was done by Zadok the priest and Nathan the prophet. This placing of oil on the forehead still takes place at the coronation of the kings and queens of England. It symbolises God's approval of the monarch and the gift of His spirit at the coronation.

Solomon's reign represents the height of Israel's wealth and power *(1 Kings 4 v 20)*. The famous piece of music by Handel called *The Arrival of the Queen of Sheba* is based upon the story of the Queen's visit to Solomon because of his fame and his achievements *(1 Kings v 10)*.

He married foreign wives to secure friendships with neighbouring countries. (His wives were the daughter of the king of Egypt, Hittite women and women from Moab, Ammon, Edom and Sidon!) He did this despite the fact that the Lord had commanded that his people should not marry into other cultures.

Solomon also used his neighbours. The Phoenicians provided the skills and materials for his building schemes and the experienced sailors for a short-lived naval experiment. He traded horses with Egypt.

But he lost the goodwill of his people by imposing upon them heavy taxes and some forced labour in order to pay for all his great schemes. As a result of this discontent, the ten northern tribes of Israel broke away from the tribes in the south and what was one nation became divided. This was viewed as a punishment sent by God for Solomon's forbidden marriages.

Questions on the Commentary

1. Apart from his wisdom, for what is King Solomon most famous?

2. Why did the people of Israel want a temple?

3. What is the word used in the commentary to describe a holy place of worship?

4. What might Solomon have asked for instead of wisdom?

5. Why did he ask for wisdom?

6. Why did the people of Israel benefit from having Jerusalem as a capital?

7. What was the *covenant box*?

8. What did Solomon gain from neighbouring countries?

9. Why, by the end of his reign, might Solomon have been thought of as not so wise?

CONTEMPORARY ISSUES

WISDOM

(i) The book of Proverbs is full of wise sayings such as:

Proverbs 15 v 1 *A gentle answer quietens anger, but a harsh one stirs it up.*

16 v 28 *Gossip is spread by wicked people; they stir up trouble and break up friendships.*

17 v 1 *Better to eat a dry crust with peace of mind than to have a banquet in a house full of trouble.*

20 v 1 *Drinking too much makes you loud and foolish. It's stupid to get drunk.*

22 v 1 *If you have to choose between a good reputation and great wealth, choose a good reputation.*

Have a look for yourself and make a note of your favourite proverbs.

(ii) Here are some wise sayings which thirteen year olds have made up themselves:

Don't cough or sneeze in other people's faces, especially if you don't know them.
Girls are more important than you think.
Life is like a choose-your-own-ending book – you can take whatever adventures you want.
Attitudes are contagious.
Laugh at other people's jokes.

1. Make up some wise sayings yourself. Choose the best sayings

    either (a) in order to produce a class display of them

    or (b) make individual cards or posters with them in the art room or ICT room.

2. Make a list of the qualities which you think are needed in a national leader.

3. Borrow CDs from the music department which contain *Zadok the Priest* and *The Arrival of the Queen of Sheba* (both tracks were composed by Handel) and listen to them as a class.

4. Divide into five groups and research different aspects of the life of the Queen to present a school assembly on Queen Elizabeth II.

Common Entrance Questions

1. (a) What did Solomon ask of God? (1)

   (b) Two women came to Solomon with a dispute. What was the reason for the dispute? (2)

   (c) What did each woman accuse the other of doing? (2)

   (d) Describe how Solomon settled the dispute. (5)

   (e) Explain why Solomon's judgement is regarded as being wise. (5)

   (f) Give examples from today's world of what you understand by wisdom. Explain why you have selected these examples. (10)

2. (a) In which city did Solomon live? (1)

   (b) What was Solomon building? (1)

   (c) Where did Solomon go to offer sacrifices, and how is this place described? (3)

   (d) What did Solomon ask for in a dream? What did God say about Solomon's request? (5)

   (e) Explain why Solomon's request was very sensible. (5)

   (f) Do you think that our country benefits from having a monarch today? (10)

Scholarship Questions

1. (a) Retell the story of how Solomon used his wisdom to judge a difficult case. (8)

   (b) What do you understand the word *wisdom* to mean? Provide plenty of examples in your answer. (12)

2. The Prince of Wales once said that he would like one of the titles of the monarch to be changed from 'Defender of the Faith' to 'Defender of Faith'.

   (a) What do you think he meant? (6)

   (b) Do you agree? Give full reasoning in your answer. (14)

3. How important is it for the monarch to be moral in his or her private life? (20)

4. A former ambassador to the Court of St James wrote the following about our monarchy:

   > With the monarchy here, it is a bit like Solomon's Temple. There is much to be penetrated before you get to the centre – long passageways, both literal and figurative, and it is an elaborate circumstance for an outsider . . . It's unusual, and there's the protocol, there are the courtiers, long passageways and carpets and chandeliers, enormous rooms and guards. That is part of the requirement and mystique of royalty.

   Give your views upon his claim that mystique is necessary in the monarchy. (20)

9

ELIJAH STORIES

ELIJAH AND THE PROPHETS OF BAAL

1 KINGS 18

The Lord sent fire down (1 Kings 18 v 38)

SUMMARY OF THE TEXT

It was the third year of the drought. King Ahab sent Obadiah his servant to search out springs and river beds for water.

Obadiah was a faithful worshipper of the Lord who had saved one hundred of the Lord's prophets from Queen Jezebel's persecution.

While searching for water, Obadiah met the prophet Elijah who immediately asked him to bring the king to him.

Obadiah could not believe his ears, as the king had already searched high and low for Elijah, and to take such a message to the king would mean, he felt, certain death!

Elijah reassured him that it was the will of God and so he took the message.

Indeed Ahab did come out to meet Elijah that day.

Elijah offered a challenge to Ahab.

He asked him to bring the 450 prophets of the god Baal and the 400 prophets of the goddess Asherah to Mount Carmel.

Once there, in front of the people, he suggested that two bulls be sacrificed but neither he nor the rival prophets would light a fire under them.

Both sides would ask their god to send fire. The one who did would be the real god.

The prophets of Baal went first, but by noon nothing had happened.

Elijah began to make fun of them and suggested that Baal was 'day dreaming, relieving himself or going on a journey!'

The prophets of Baal then prayed more loudly and began to cut themselves until the middle of the afternoon.

Still nothing happened.

Elijah then called the people round him, took twelve stones (one for each of the twelve tribes of Israel), built an altar, dug a trench round it, prepared a bull and then had it and the wood beneath it covered in water.

At the hour of the afternoon sacrifice, Elijah prayed to the Lord who sent fire down which burned up the sacrifice, the wood and the stones, scorched the earth and dried up the water in the trench.

The people then threw themselves on the ground and worshipped the Lord.

Elijah then ordered the people to seize the prophets of Baal and to kill them, which they did.

Elijah then went to the top of Mount Carmel where he asked his servant to go and look towards the sea.

Six times the servant returned without having seen anything.

Then, after the seventh trip, he returned and reported seeing a little cloud no bigger than a man's hand.

Shortly afterwards the sky was covered in dark clouds and heavy rain began to fall.

Ahab got back in his chariot, but the Lord's power came upon Elijah who fastened his clothes round his waist and ran ahead of Ahab back to Jezreel.

COMMENTARY ON THE TEXT

v 4 . . . and when Jezebel was killing the Lord's prophets . . .

Because of Jezebel's wickedness in Bible stories, the name Jezebel has come to our language to describe a scheming, evil woman who will do anything to serve her own purposes. (For an example read the story of Naboth's vineyard, *1 Kings v 21.*)

Jezebel was from Phoenicia and, when she married Ahab, she insisted that he and his people worshipped her god, Melcart, and she encouraged worship of the Canaanite baals also. She had murdered as many of the prophets of God as could not escape or find hiding. One hundred were saved through the secret help of Ahab's chamberlain Obadiah.

v 19 The Challenge to the Prophets of Baal . . .

The great influence of Jezebel is shown by the number of the prophets of her gods: 450 prophets of Baal and 400 prophets of the goddess Asherah. Mount Carmel was chosen because it was a sacred place for both the Phoenicians and the Israelites. But the people then had to choose between the rival religions. They could now no longer try to keep both going at the same time, as many of them had been doing.

v 27 At noon Elijah started making fun of them . . .

This must have made their dancing and shouting even more frenzied.

v 28 *. . . according to their ritual . . .*

A ritual is a ceremony which is regularly repeated. This verse suggests that cutting themselves – offering their own pain and blood to Baal – was something they often did.

v 35 *The water ran down round the altar and filled the trench.*

At first sight this looks like an act to make God's power seem even stronger – that he could bring fire to soaked wood! However, it is also likely to be part of a ritual to ask for rain to end the drought. For in *v 42*, Elijah bowed down to the ground *with his head between his knees*. So, with his own body, he was making the shape of the cloud which the next moment he asked his servant to go and look for in the sky.

Questions on the Commentary

1. What does it mean to call a woman a *Jezebel*?

2. What evidence is there in the text to show the extent of the influence which Jezebel had on the nation?

3. In which ways was Obadiah brave?

4. Explain the meaning of the word *ritual*.

5. Why did Elijah add water when it was his turn to take the challenge?

THE STILL SMALL VOICE

1 KINGS 19 vv 1–18

SUMMARY OF THE TEXT

When Jezebel heard from Ahab that Elijah had put all her prophets to death, Elijah had to flee for his life.

He was filled with despair.

While he slept, an angel gave him bread and water and told him that he needed to build himself up for the forty-day journey to Mount Sinai.

On arrival at Mount Sinai, the holy mountain, Elijah went into a cave to spend the night.

The next day the Lord asked him why he had come.

Elijah told the Lord how the people of Israel had broken their covenant by killing the prophets and tearing down the altars of the Lord.

God then told Elijah to stand on the mountain top.

The Lord then sent a wind so strong that it shattered the rocks, but the Lord was not in the wind.

This was followed by an earthquake, but the Lord was not in the earthquake.

There was a fire, but the Lord was not in the fire.

After the fire, there was the soft whisper of a voice.

The voice said to Elijah, 'Elijah, what are you doing here?'

Elijah again told the Lord he was in despair about the people breaking their covenant.

He was the only prophet of the Lord left and now his life was in danger.

The Lord then instructed Elijah to anoint two new kings to kill those who had been unfaithful to the Lord.

Seven thousand people would be left alive – those who had been faithful and who had not bowed down to the Baals.

The Lord also told Elijah to anoint Elisha as his successor.

COMMENTARY ON THE TEXT

The great day of Carmel did not have a lasting effect on the people. The prophets of the Lord had to remain in hiding.

Elijah felt completely alone, without support, and he desperately needed encouragement.

After a day's journey he was in despair.

v 5 . . . *'Wake up and eat.'*

This food from the angel renewed Elijah's courage and his will to go on.

v 8 . . . *and the food gave him enough strength to walk forty days to Sinai, the holy mountain.*

Mount Sinai was the mountain upon which God had revealed himself to Moses and where Moses had been given the Law.

It was God's special dwelling place. In the state Elijah was in, Sinai was the most natural place for him to look for God's presence and guidance.

v 13 When Elijah heard it (the soft whisper of a voice), *he covered his face with his cloak* . . .

Elijah waited on the word of the Lord and covered his face because man could not look upon the Lord and live.

Wind, earthquake and fire: none of these great forces of nature, outside of him, contained the message which Elijah needed.

91

God's presence lay inside him.

God's quiet voice spoke to him to renew his faith and to strengthen Elijah's purpose.

CONTEMPORARY ISSUES

COURAGE

War brings out the worst and the best in people. It would be all too easy to think only of the evil – the terrible atrocities that one human being can commit against another man, woman or even child. But when I am tempted to think only of evil in man, I remember the countless selfless acts of courage which men and women showed to save others. The captain of a tiny destroyer who turned her round to take on a giant German battleship in order to buy just twenty more minutes of time for the convoy he was protecting. The young women, like Sadie Talbot, who drove ambulances in the First World War, ferrying the wounded soldiers across the ruined countryside of Flanders, often under continuous bombardment, to a field dressing station.

Use the school library and other appropriate resources to research:

- information for a school assembly on the courage of women in war

- from *Naught for Your Comfort* by Fr. Trevor Huddleston, a talk on his work as a priest in Sophiatown, South Africa in the apartheid years

- the work of Martin Luther King or Nelson Mandela

Common Entrance Questions

1. (a) Who was Jezebel? (1)

   (b) What was Obadiah's job and whom did he worship? (2)

   (c) What had Obadiah done to save the Lord's prophets? (2)

   (d) Explain why Obadiah was reluctant to tell Ahab that Elijah had returned. (5)

   (e) Explain why Ahab referred to Elijah as 'the worst trouble maker in Israel'. (5)

   (f) 'Elijah the troublemaker would have plenty to complain about today.' Do you agree? Give reasons to support your answer. (10)

2. (a) Who had brought the worship of Baal to Israel? (1)

   (b) Elijah set up a competition between the prophets of Baal and himself. Where did this competition take place? (2)

   (c) What was the aim of the competition? (2)

   (d) Describe briefly what happened. (5)

   (e) Explain, as fully as you can, what this story tells us about the character of Elijah. (5)

   (f) It is often said that we worship many 'false gods' today. What might these be, and why do we worship them? (10)

3. (a) Why did Elijah flee into the wilderness? (1)

   (b) What did Elijah say to God when he sat under the tree? (2)

   (c) Which **two** items did the Angel bring to Elijah? (2)

   (d) Describe the first **three** dramatic events which took place while Elijah stood before the Lord on the top of the mountain. (5)

   (e) What was the fourth event? Explain why you think God came to Elijah in this way. (5)

   (f) In which different ways do you think God might speak to people today? (10)

Scholarship Questions

1. Was it right for Elijah to encourage the people to slay the prophets of Baal? (20)

2. How can all religions be true? (20)

3. In what sense are there prophets of Baal today? (20)

4. The writer and broadcaster Ludovic Kennedy said the following:

    My objection to many so-called Christians is that some are the most intolerant people I know. These are the people who call for the return of the rope and the lash. Throughout history, and particularly today, I believe religion has been inclined, on balance, to do more harm than good.

    Write your opinion in full about these views. (20)

10

THE PROPHET AMOS

THE MESSAGE OF THE PROPHET AMOS

AMOS 5

A NOTE ON THE ROLE OF AN OLD TESTAMENT PROPHET

Today we think of prophecy as being about foretelling the future, perhaps by palm-reading, astrology or gazing into a crystal ball. The Old Testament prophet did none of these things. He was quite simply a messenger of God. His work was to speak God's news to his people. Often the prophet had to be very brave. He might, for example, have to tell the king that God was now on the side of his enemy because he and his people had worshipped other gods.

AMOS

Amos lived in the eighth century BC as a shepherd when God called him to be a prophet. It was a period during the reign of King Jeroboam, when the people of Israel were wealthy and kept their religious observances well.

Amos lived at a time when there had been a long period of peace and prosperity. There was a large number of slaves and poor whose work supported the wealthy. However, it was also a time of corruption in business life and in the courts bribes were commonplace.

SUMMARY OF THE TEXT

The words of the chapter are the words which Amos spoke to the people of his day.

His message was that the people had become too comfortable and complacent.

Although, on the face of it, they seemed to be fulfilling their religious rituals, they did nothing to help the poor and needy or to see that there was proper justice for all.

They looked forward to the 'Day of the Lord' but Amos warned them it was not to be a day of celebration: it would be a day of God's judgement for them.

COMMENTARY ON THE TEXT

The prophets often likened the people of Israel to a woman *(v 2 Virgin Israel)*. This provided a metaphor for God's relationship with them. They were His bride. God had loved 'her' and had done wonderful things in the past for 'her', such as setting 'her' free from slavery in Egypt.

By worshipping other gods, Israel had proven herself unfaithful to God, so God would abandon her. In *vv 26* and *27* Amos points to the time of exile, when a conquered Israel would be taken in captivity into a foreign land. (This happened when the Jewish people were taken to Babylonia in 597 and 586 BC.)

v 4 . . . Beersheba . . . Bethel . . . Gilgal . . .

These are places where the people of Israel had set up altars so that they could make sacrifices to keep God happy with their offerings. Amos told them not to bother because God was so unhappy with them!

v 8 The Lord made the stars, the Pleiades and Orion.

Like the *Book of Psalms* in the Old Testament, the prophets often reminded the people of the mighty creative power of God in His great works of creation – the stars, the mountains and hills, the raging of the seas etc.

v 18 . . . the day of the Lord

The people thought that would be a marvellous religious festival, bringing a great feast which they were looking forward to. Amos told them that this day would be a day of judgement when they would be doomed for all the sins they had committed. Amos lists the sins:

vv 11–12 You have oppressed the poor and robbed them of their grain . . . you persecute good men, take bribes and prevent the poor from getting justice in the courts.

vv 16–18 The idea of punishment would amaze them because these wealthy people thought that they had done all the right things for their religion which the Lord required. However, in the verses which follow, Amos told them in plain language what God thought about their religion!

vv 21–24 The Lord says 'I hate your religious festivals; I cannot stand them! When you bring me . . . offerings . . . I will not accept them; I will not accept the animals . . . offerings. Stop your noisy songs; I do not want to listen to your harps. Instead, let justice flow like a stream and righteousness like a river that never goes dry.'

God did not want costly and complicated ceremonies from these people. He would much rather have right conduct than correct ceremonies.

But let Justice roll down like waters . . . is an often quoted verse (in an older translation) from this passage. It has been used by black Civil Rights preachers, such as Martin Luther King. Before the 1960s in some of the southern states of the USA, black people were denied equal rights to white. These words, which Amos used on behalf of the downtrodden poor of his day, made a great sound in the mouths of powerful black preachers as they felt that God supported their movement.

Questions on the Commentary

1. What was Amos before he was called to be a prophet?

2. What was the work of a prophet?

3. Describe the time during which Amos lived.

4. Imagine you are a reporter at the time of Amos. Write a brief newspaper article about his message to the nation. You can choose whether you work for *The Sun* or *The Times*.

5. Why would the people be surprised at Amos' message?

6. Which **two** meanings for 'The Day of the Lord' are present in the text?

7. Why does Amos tell the people that God hates their religious rituals?

8. Find the quotation from Amos in Martin Luther King's *I have a Dream* speech. The full text of this can be found at http://www.stanford.edn/group/king/frequentdics

AMOS AND AMAZIAH

AMOS 7 vv 10–17

SUMMARY OF THE TEXT

Amos' message of God's judgement against the people of Israel angered Amaziah.

He was one of the priests of the Lord who worked from Bethel. Bethel was one of the shrines to which the people could go to sacrifice an animal.

Amaziah sent a full report to King Jeroboam of Israel, accusing Amos of treason and plotting against the King.

Amaziah told Amos directly that he was fed up with Amos' dreadful preaching.

He told him to pack up and to go and be a prophet in Judah.

Bethel was the national shrine, the king's place of worship, and not the place for the sort of words which Amos was using!

Amos replied that he was not the sort of prophet who could be hired!

He had been a herdsman who, while taking care of his fig trees, had been called by the Lord to be a prophet, because Amaziah had been linked to *false* religion.

Amos delivered news from God of a terrible punishment to Amaziah and his family.

Also Amos told him that the people of Israel would be sent into exile from their own land to another country.

COMMENTARY ON THE TEXT

v 12 Amaziah then said to Amos, 'That's enough, prophet. Go back to Judah and do your preaching there. Let them pay you for it.'

Amaziah had a comfortable position as priest at the royal place of worship. The last thing he wanted was Amos spreading doom and gloom and upsetting the king and the people.

As far as Amaziah was concerned, in his very important and comfortable royal shrine, religion was about offering the right sacrifice at Bethel. It was not about caring for the poor nor about making sure that there was justice in the land. The very last thing he wanted was this upstart Amos 'rocking the boat' in the name of religion!

He was sneering when he called Amos a 'prophet'.

Amos, he said, should get back to Judah where he came from and he should leave the Northern Kingdom of Israel and its religious health to him!

v 14 '*I am not the kind of prophet who prophesies for pay.*'

Amos was anxious to tell Amaziah that he was not some sort of fortune-teller who could be bought. He did not prophesy for a living. He was not a professional. There was no gain for him from what he said.

Amos was not even a prophet from his own choice. He was leading the simple (poor) life of a herdsman, caring for his figs, when his call came from God. After that he could do no other than say, 'This is the word of the Lord!' as he delivered God's judgement upon the people of Israel.

v 17 . . . *and you yourself will die in a heathen country.*

These terrible words of judgement on Amaziah and his family, pronounced by Amos, showed Amos as completely fearless as he had the last word (words in fact from God) in this row with Amaziah.

To summarise

In the Bible a **prophet** is quite simply someone who speaks God's word and brings a contemporary message from God to His people.

Amos' experience as a biblical prophet was typical in that:

- he did not choose the job – God chose him

- because his message was unpopular, he was unpopular

- he had to have great courage to deliver God's message

Look for the parallels in the lives of Elijah, Jeremiah, Jonah and John the Baptist.

CONTEMPORARY ISSUES

THE POOR IN SOCIETY

Like Amos, David Sheppard (Bishop of Liverpool 1974-1997) spoke out about the conditions in which the poor had to live. He believed that the church in Liverpool should take a special interest in how poor people could be supported, better housed and given more opportunities for employment – especially the young. In his book *Bias to the Poor* he spoke of the achievements of young people living on a housing estate.

I was surprised and delighted to see fifteen and sixteen-year-old boys, a normally self-conscious age, dancing their hearts out in scenes from 'Grease'. How had this happened? It was because of a young teacher, an old boy of the school; he had qualified as a teacher elsewhere and had now come back to teach in his old school. He lived on the estate like other teachers and nurses who had grown up there and were determined to stay and help their own.

Another writer explains why these estates produced problems.

Immediately after the Second World War, new council house estates were built on the outskirts of cities. On these estates were large tower blocks and in the beginning too few shops. But they were a disaster right from the start. The people who were moved to them had been uprooted from neighbourhoods where their families had lived for years. Those roots were broken up in the move.

In their old neighbourhoods, married couples would just move one or two streets away from their parents. This meant that they were supported by them with their babies and the upbringing of their children. The old terraced houses were rightly called slums but they housed communities of people who cared about each other. Neighbours would keep an eye on children, give you food if you were hard up, not to mention help with childbirth or the laying out of the dead. When you lived on the twenty-sixth floor of a tower block, the only neighbours that were visible to you were the seagulls.

1. Why were the teenage boys prepared to dance?

2. Why were tower blocks a disaster for poor people?

3. Imagine you have just been moved into a tower block. Write a letter to your old neighbours who have decided to stay where they are as long as they can.

4. Find out what is meant by a *slum*. What were the advantages of living in the old neighbourhoods?

5. Research the work of the Church in the inner city by writing to the Dioceses of London, Southwark, Leeds, Liverpool or Birmingham for information.

6. Prepare an assembly talk on the work of the *Salvation Army* among the homeless in London.

7. *Speakers' Corner* in Hyde Park is often thought of as a place for today's prophets. Every Sunday many people stand on a soapbox, gather a crowd around them and, with lots of energy and enthusiasm in their voice, tell all who will listen what is wrong with our society.

   Prepare a short speech about something in your school or our society which you think needs changing. Then go outside at break time with your friends and start a *Speakers' Corner*.

8. Design a poster for a local charity of your choice.

Common Entrance Questions

1. (a) To whom did Amos prophesy? (1)

   (b) Why did Amos describe his message as a 'funeral song'? (2)

   (c) What did the people believe would happen on the day of the Lord? (2)

   (d) Why do you think that the poor received special attention in his message? (5)

   (e) Explain why you think Amos criticised the religion of his day. (5)

   (f) If Amos were alive today, what message do you think he would give to us? (10)

2. (a) What did Amaziah the priest tell Amos to do? (1)

   (b) Amos did not describe himself as the kind of prophet who prophesies for pay. What did he say he was? (2)

   (c) What did Amos say would happen to Israel? (2)

   (d) What did Amos say about the treatment of the poor? (5)

   (e) Explain what Amos said about the religion of his day. (5)

   (f) Imagine that Amos was around today. What would he say about society and religion in the twenty-first century? (10)

Scholarship Questions

1. Should bishops ever speak out about the failings of a government to meet the needs of the poor? (20)

2. If you were given one minute to speak to the nation on prime-time television, what would you say? (20)

3. What needs changing in our society? (20)

4. 'Fanaticism is the enemy of true religion.' Do you agree? (20)

5. 'The clergy should spend less time talking about the ills of society and spend more time getting people back into their empty pews.' Write your views about this newspaper comment. (20)

NEW TESTAMENT TEXTS

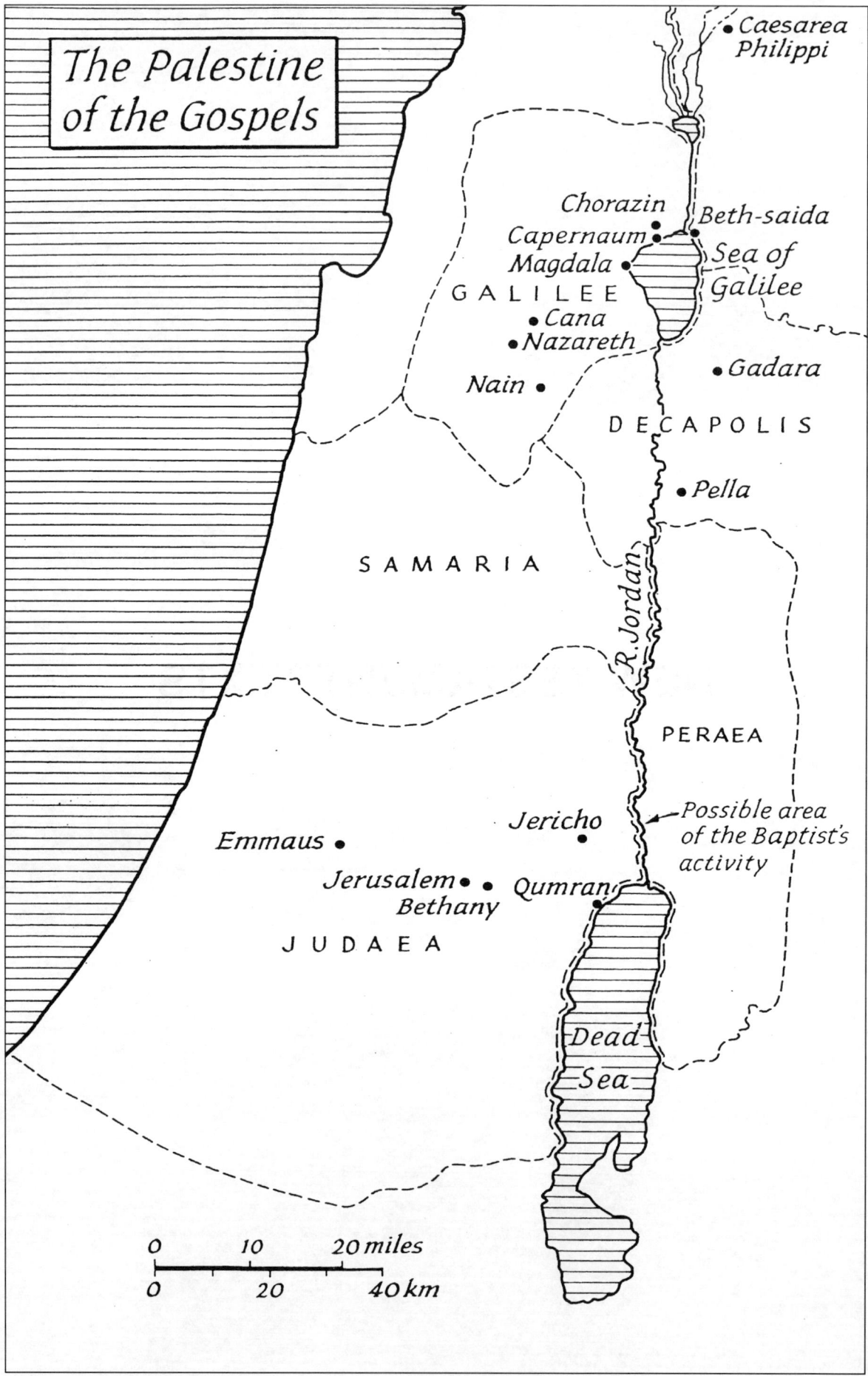

The Palestine
of the Gospels

Caesarea
Philippi

Chorazin
Capernaum
Magdala
Beth-saida
Sea of
Galilee

GALILEE

Cana
Nazareth

Gadara

Nain

DECAPOLIS

Pella

SAMARIA

R. Jordan

PERAEA

Jericho

Possible area
of the Baptist's
activity

Emmaus

Jerusalem
Bethany
Qumran

JUDAEA

Dead
Sea

0   10   20 miles
0   20   40 km

INTRODUCTION

JESUS IN HISTORY

The theme of the New Testament

For Christians, the New Testament is the second part of the story of God's involvement with mankind. Part one (the Old Testament) is about God using His prophets to try to put right His relationship with the Jewish people.

Part two, then, is chiefly concerned with the story of Jesus who, Christians believe, completely restored this relationship, not only for the Jews, but for all mankind. One of the earliest Christian writers, St Paul, puts the same idea in these words:

> *For just as all people die because of their union with Adam, in the same way all will be raised to life because of their union with Christ.* (1 Corinthians 15 v 22)

The books of the New Testament

The New Testament consists of a collection of books originally written in Greek. They were circulated among believers as they were written, between AD 40 and AD 100, and were gradually assembled between about AD 130 and AD 350.

The books of the New Testament are:

- the *Gospels* of *Matthew, Mark, Luke* and *John*

- the *Acts of the Apostles*

- a collection of letters, known as *Epistles*, which had been sent to support and guide the newly-founded Christian communities

- the *Book of the Revelation of St John*

Other sources

Jesus lived in Palestine. He was born and died a Jew. He lived during a period when his homeland was part of the Roman Empire. His people, for the most part, were offended by the presence of these Roman 'foreigners' on their God-given 'holy' land. Throughout his life, therefore, he was surrounded by political tension.

The Gospels are not our only source of information about this period in history. The Jews and the Romans kept records of this period too. It is interesting to compare the names of officials given in their documents with those in the Gospels. The results not only prove that Jesus actually existed but also provide some idea of the dates of his birth and death.

Below are some of the names of officials given in *Luke 3 vv 1–6*. Alongside are the dates for these people which can be found in Roman and Jewish records.

Tiberius Caesar

Luke dates the start of John the Baptist's preaching as in the fifteenth year of the rule of Tiberius. Clearly, Tiberius' life is well documented in Roman history. However, if the Jewish religious calendar is used to measure fifteen years of his rule, a date of AD 27 emerges.

Pontius Pilate

Roman records list him as Procurator of Judaea from AD 26–36.

Herod the Great

Jewish records tell us that he died in 4 BC. One of his sons, Herod Antipas, ruled Galilee until AD 39.

Annas

High Priest of the Temple at Jerusalem AD 6–15

Caiphas

High Priest from AD 18–36

These dates lead to a best guess for Jesus' life dating from around 5 BC to around AD 33.

The Jesus of the Gospels

The word *Gospel* means *Good News*. The writers wanted to share what they believed to be the good news about Jesus. The purpose of each writer was to convince the reader that Jesus was God's *Messiah* (Hebrew word) or *Christ* (in the Greek of the Gospels).

The *Gospels* are not biographies of Jesus. They contain very few details of his life. (*Mark* and *John* do not provide any birth stories, for example.) The writing they contain is mainly about Jesus' teaching and his miracles. The only period of his life outlined in any detail in the *Gospels* is his final week on Earth which tells of his arrest, trial, death and resurrection.

However, in trying to prove in their writing that Jesus was the expected Messiah, the Gospel writers faced the same problem which Jesus faced when he taught his fellow Jews. They had come to believe that the longed-for Messiah would be a warrior king who would rid them of the Romans. This was clearly not so.

The word *Messiah* means *Anointed One*. When put into the Greek language, *Messiah* becomes *Christ*. So *Jesus Christ* means *Jesus Messiah*. It is a bit like *Tony, Prime Minister* or *Rowan, Archbishop*. The first part is a name, the second a title.

The title *Anointed One* was also used of King David, Israel's greatest warrior king. It is not surprising, therefore, that at the time of Jesus the hope would be for a new leader, like David, who would do with the Romans what David did with the Philistines.

The *Gospels*, however, show Jesus to be a teacher much more concerned with the Kingdom of God than the Kingdom of Rome. Jesus' parables were aimed at people discovering the nearness of God's kingdom in their everyday lives. There was never a hint that they should take up arms to sort out the problems they had with this world.

Jesus' purpose was clearly not to lead a revolutionary movement to rid the country of Romans by violence. An organisation to do this did exist at the time of Jesus and its followers were called the *Zealots*. (This name is still used today to describe a fanatical believer in a cause.) Some people suggest that the disciple who betrayed Jesus, Judas Iscariot, was a Zealot. By handing Jesus over for arrest, he hoped an uprising would follow, but it did not, and when he saw Jesus die, he hanged himself.

Jesus' ministry

The word *ministry* means the work of serving others. It was Jesus' aim to serve God by serving mankind. This he did by means of his words and actions.

It is clear from the Gospels that Jesus grew up as any Jewish boy did at that time. He followed the trade of his father and attended the synagogue on the Sabbath. At the proper times he and his family would journey to the Temple at Jerusalem to offer the correct animal sacrifices. He would know well the law, customs and traditions of his people.

At about the age of thirty he knew he was called by God to leave his family and begin his ministry. The sign of this beginning was his baptism by John in the River Jordan. After this he spent forty days in the wilderness thinking about how he should go about the great work of ministry to which God had called him.

Opposition to Jesus

In the chapters which follow, clear answers will emerge to two very important questions.

- How is it that Jesus, who talked of love and healed the sick, ended up condemned to death?

- If Jesus was God's Messiah, why did so many people not recognise him?

Jesus' impact

Whatever the people of his time thought of Jesus, one thing is certain: no one else in history has had the same impact on humanity. Whether we believe in him or not, the date will always be measured from his birth. These ideas have been expressed in the writing below.

These words are often entitled *One Solitary Life*. The author is unknown.

Here is a man who was born in an obscure village, the child of a peasant woman. He worked in a carpenter's shop until he was thirty and then for three years he was a travelling preacher. He had no qualifications but himself. While still a young man, the tide of popular opinion turned against him. His friends, the twelve men who had learned so much from him and promised him loyalty, ran away and left him. He went through a mockery of a trial: he was nailed to a cross between two thieves; when he was dead, he was taken down and laid in a borrowed grave through the pity of a friend. Yet I am well within the mark when I say that all the armies that ever marched, and all the parliaments that ever sat and all the kings that ever reigned, put together, have not affected the life of man upon this earth as has this one solitary life.

Questions on the Introduction

1. In which language was the New Testament written?

2. Find out which animal has become a symbol for each *Gospel* writer. In art, use these symbols to produce a work entitled *Good News*.

3. What other sources are used to provide information about the time at which Jesus lived?

4. If you were given the task of writing a biography of Jesus, what more would you like to know about him?

5. Use the library to find out more about the Zealots.

6. Fill in the missing words from these sentences.

    (i)   Jesus lived in ....

    (ii) Jesus was a .... by birth and religion.

    (iii) Each Saturday he would worship with the other men in the

          ....

7. Fill in the names of the men who held positions of power during Jesus' life.

    (i)   .... died in 4 BC.

          His son .... ruled Galilee until AD 39.

    (ii) Until AD 36 the .... of Judea was Pontius

          ....

    (iii) The most probable dates for Jesus' life are .... BC to

          AD ....

8. What is the meaning of the word *Messiah*?

9. Read carefully the *One Solitary Life* paragraph above and list at least **four** ways in which you think the life of Jesus has influenced our world.

1

THE TEMPTATIONS OF JESUS

LUKE 4 vv 1–13

Order this stone to turn into bread (Luke 4 v 3)

SUMMARY OF THE TEXT

Jesus spent forty days without food in the wilderness, during which he was tempted by the devil in three ways to:

- turn stones into bread

- accept power over mankind in return for worshipping only the Devil and not God

- throw himself off the highest pinnacle of the Temple

To each of these temptations Jesus replied:

- 'Man shall not live by bread alone.'

- 'You shall worship the Lord thy God and Him only shalt thou serve.'

- 'You shall not tempt the Lord thy God.'

COMMENTARY ON THE TEXT

The Devil

In another part of the New Testament, the Devil is described as an angel who rebelled against God and so was cast out of God's favour. He is seen as the cause of evil in the world by tempting humans to do evil rather than to do good.

v 3 . . . order this stone to turn into bread.

This temptation is not just about satisfying Jesus' hunger. That the Messiah should bring food for his people was a very old idea. Here, Jesus was being tempted to produce food for the people, as Moses did when the people were starving in the desert. In Jesus' time, many people did not have enough to eat, so to provide food for them would be a way of attracting people and keeping them.

However, Jesus knew that the most important need his people had was not their hunger for food but a hunger for spiritual truths about God.

v 7 All this will be yours, then, if you worship me.

At the time of Jesus a group of men called Zealots met to plot violence against the Romans – a sort of guerilla band. They saw this as a 'Holy War'. In their eyes the Romans were defiling God's land by their very presence. The occupation by the Roman Empire was for them not just humiliating but, much worse, it was an offence against God – a blasphemy.

Jesus knew it would be very easy to rouse the people and be like a Zealot, perhaps even join with them and, by a violent revolution, join the attacks against Rome.

This is what the second temptation offered Jesus: a chance to seize power, using his great skills of drawing crowds to hear him.

v 9 If you are God's son, throw yourself down from here.

From the highest point of the Temple – the top of the royal porch (the pinnacle) – to the Kidron valley below is about 150 metres. Jesus knew that he had the power to leap from the top and survive. So it was a real temptation for him to do this and leave the people in no doubt that he was God's Anointed One – the hoped-for Messiah. But that was the trouble.

If he did this, there would be no possibility for doubt. But then, there would be no room for **faith**. The people would have had no choice but to believe and that was not what

113

Jesus wanted. He wanted the people to **choose** to believe in him. Jesus' teaching through parables was almost always designed to provoke people into making a choice. Magical acts such as surviving a 150 metre-leap would leave them with no choice.

v 13 *When the Devil finished tempting Jesus in every way, he left him for a while.*

This verse shows that there were not just three temptations during the forty days. The words *every way* also open up the humanity of Jesus. They mean in every way in which we are tempted. *For a while* also shows that the temptations did not stop when he left the wilderness.

Questions on the Commentary

1. Outline why each of the offers made to Jesus were real temptations for him.

2. Which words in the passage indicate that this was not the only occasion when Jesus was tempted to do wrong?

3. Who were the Zealots?

CONTEMPORARY ISSUES

GOOD VERSUS EVIL

James remembered that when he was ten, whenever his father said to him, 'If you do that one more time I will give you a smack,' James would do whatever it was one more time for the thrill of the chase around the house. He said he could never resist the temptation to do the naughty thing one more time. The smack was worth the excitement of the chase!

Why are things we are not supposed to do often attractive or even irresistible? Is it like the forbidden fruit of the Garden of Eden? Things become more attractive when they are forbidden.

The following poem is written by a man remembering his Saturday morning visits to the cinema in the 1950s when he was a boy. He thinks of the cowboy films which were always 'the goodies versus the baddies'. The good cowboys used to be always in white and the bad ones were dressed in black and even rode black horses.

The poet writes:

> But of the flickering myths themselves
> Not much remains. The hero was
> A smily, wide-brimmed hat, a shape
> Astride the arched white stallion.
> The villain's horse and hat were black.
> Disbelief did not exist
> And laundered virtue always won
> With quicker gun and harder fist
> And all of us applauded it.
> Yet I remember moments when
> In solitude I'd find myself
> Brooding on the sooty man.

1. As a class, discuss the meaning of:

   (i) *flickering myths*

   (ii) *disbelief did not exist*

   (iii) *laundered virtue*

   (iv) *I'd find myself brooding on the sooty man*

2. Make a list of the names of any villains from films or novels which you can think of. Are there any you can remember who were attractive to you in any way? If so, why?

3. In groups of four, take it in turns to remember times when you did not resist temptation. Try and explain why.

4. Just as in cowboy films, Darth Vadar and the Emperor in the *Star Wars* films are dressed in black, whereas Luke Skywalker is in white. Why do you think that these colours are not used to represent good and bad people today?

5. Can you think of a story you have read or a film you have seen where evil defeats good? If not, do you think that some stories should end that way sometimes?

Common Entrance Questions

1. (a) Where did the temptations take place? (1)

   (b) How long was Jesus there? (1)

   (c) In which ways did the Devil tempt Jesus? (3)

   (d) Describe how Jesus replied to the Devil's temptations. (5)

   (e) What do you think this story is trying to say about Jesus and the way he understood his work? Give your reasons. (5)

   (f) 'Temptations are the hurdles upon which we build our character.' Do you agree with this statement? Give full reasons in your answer. (10)

2. (a) From where had Jesus returned just before his temptations? (1)

   (b) Who led Jesus and where did he lead him? (2)

   (c) For how long was Jesus tempted and what did he eat during that time? (2)

   (d) Briefly describe the three temptations? (5)

   (e) Explain the meaning behind the temptations. (5)

   (f) 'Good people always resist temptations.' Do you agree? Give full reasons to support your answer. (10)

Scholarship Questions

1. (a) Outline the options which Jesus considered during his forty days in the wilderness and explain why they were real temptations for him. (8)

    (b) Oscar Wilde wrote: 'I can resist anything except temptation.' Do you think this is generally true of us all? (12)

2. Is it necessary to believe in the Devil to explain the existence of evil in the world? (20)

3. What do you think the consequences would have been for Jesus if he had not resisted the third temptation? (20)

4. Is it only fear of punishment which helps us resist temptation? (20)

JESUS AND THE OUTCASTS

ZACCHAEUS

LUKE 19 vv 1–10

SUMMARY OF THE TEXT

On his way through Jericho, Jesus noticed a small man named Zacchaeus in a tree.

Zacchaeus had climbed there to get a better view of Jesus.

When Jesus saw Zacchaeus, he invited himself into Zacchaeus' home.

This caused upset among some bystanders because Zacchaeus worked for the Romans as chief tax-collector.

Zacchaeus gladly welcomed Jesus into his home.

He was so moved by the experience that he promised to give away half his goods to the poor and to give back four times the money to anyone he had cheated in the past.

COMMENTARY ON THE TEXT

As a tax-collector, Zacchaeus would be hated as a traitor by most of his fellow Jews. The fact that most of the tax-collectors also cheated and stole from their fellow countrymen made things worse. So Zacchaeus would not have been spoken to, would not have been allowed in the synagogue or been invited into anyone's home. No one would enter his home, either. Even to venture into the crowd as he did was risky and to climb a tree was foolhardy in the extreme. There would always be someone ready to recognise him and cause trouble.

Taking this risk was a measure of just how much he wanted to see Jesus and find out more about his teaching. He must have nearly fallen out of the tree in amazement when Jesus invited himself to his home!

Zacchaeus' immediate and enthusiastic 'yes' to Jesus' urgent 'make haste!' request was what Jesus wanted from everyone who wished to follow him. It also became the moment of repentance for Zacchaeus, the moment when Zacchaeus turned away from his old ways and promised to make a new start.

v 9 *Jesus said to him, 'Salvation has come to this house today, for this man, also, is a descendant of Abraham.'*

Abraham was thought of as the father of the Jewish nation. God made a covenant (promise) with him that if Abraham worshipped only Him, then Abraham would father a great nation – the Jewish people – who would forever think of themselves as sons and daughters of Abraham, the children of God's promise. In this story Jesus brought back (saved) Zacchaeus whose work had made him an outcast from this large family of Abraham: the Jews.

Salvation is when a person is brought back into a right relationship with God. He or she feels close to God again and not distanced from Him because of sin (wrongdoing).

The truth that God is near and is there, for non-Jews (Gentiles) as well as for Jews, is part of the Good News that the Gospel writers wanted to share.

After Jesus' death, his followers claimed that anyone who believed that he was *The Christ* would be saved. So, within about twenty years after the time of Jesus, Paul wrote in his letter to Jesus' followers in Thessalonica:

God did not choose us to suffer his anger, but to possess salvation through our Lord Jesus Christ. (1 Thessalonians 5 v 9)

LEVI :

MARK 2 vv 13–17

SUMMARY OF THE TEXT

This passage begins with Jesus teaching large crowds by the lakeside. Jesus then moved on.

On the way he saw Levi at his seat in the Custom House.

Jesus invited Levi to follow him.

Jesus then had a meal in Levi's house.

The other guests included other outcasts from the Jewish community. Some teachers of the Law, who were also Pharisees, saw this and commented upon the bad company Jesus kept.

Jesus overheard the conversation and said to them that people who are well do not need a doctor; he had come to bring back to God those who were not well in their relationship with him.

COMMENTARY ON THE TEXT

Despite his regular arguments with the religious leaders, Jesus clearly attracted crowds wherever he went to speak. Those who followed him regularly and tried to keep his teaching were called *disciples*. However, there were twelve men who were especially called by Jesus to follow him. They were called *Apostles*. This word comes from the Greek word *apostolos* – meaning *one who is sent*. Jesus did send them to teach about God's Kingdom, to heal the sick and to cast out demons, just as he had done.

In *St Matthew's* version of this story *(Matthew 9 vv 9–13)* the name *Matthew* is substituted for *Levi*. This would make Levi one of the twelve Apostles – although his name does not appear in lists of the Twelve elsewhere in the *Gospels*. However, Matthew's name does appear in the list of the twelve Apostles, so Christians think of Matthew and Levi as the same tax- collector. This means then that the call of Levi was the same as the call of the Apostle Matthew. He, of course, would have faced all the same social problems which Zacchaeus faced.

120

v 15 . . . *outcasts* . . .

These were people who deliberately did not try to keep the Jewish laws.

THE WOMAN AND SIMON THE PHARISEE

LUKE 7 vv 36–50

SUMMARY OF THE TEXT

While Jesus was a guest in the house of Simon the Pharisee, a woman who had a reputation for leading a sinful life began washing Jesus' feet with her tears.

After drying them, she poured perfume on them.

Jesus knew that Simon was thinking, 'If this man really were a prophet, he would know who this woman is who is touching him; he would know what kind of sinful life she lives!'

Jesus then told Simon a parable about two men who owed money to a moneylender.

One owed five hundred silver coins, the other fifty.

Neither could repay, so the lender cancelled both debts.

Jesus finished the parable by asking Simon which of the debtors would love the moneylender most.

Simon replied, 'I suppose . . . the one who was forgiven more.'

Jesus then pointed out that as a host, Simon had neither offered water for Jesus to bathe his feet nor had he given Jesus a kiss, yet the woman had not stopped kissing his feet.

Nor had Simon offered him olive oil for his head, yet the woman had put perfume on Jesus' head.

Jesus said that the great love which the woman had lavished upon him had proven that the woman's many sins had been forgiven.

Those who have been forgiven little, show only a little love.

Jesus then told the woman that her sins were forgiven.

She had been saved by her faith and she could go in peace.

The other dinner guests said, 'Who is this, who even forgives sins?'

COMMENTARY ON THE TEXT

v 36 . . . *a Pharisee* . . .

The Pharisees were part of the much-respected religious establishment of Jesus' time. They were experts in Jewish law and acted as guardians of Jewish religion and customs at a time when the Jews were surrounded by other cultures.

Simon clearly had enough respect for Jesus to invite him for a meal, yet the welcome seems to have been formal, not warm: no kiss, footbath or perfume – little gestures of the time which would have conveyed warmth.

v 38 . . . *and a woman who had lived a sinful life* . . . *stood behind Jesus, by his feet, crying and wetting his feet with her tears.*

At such a meal the Pharisee's door would have been open, to allow beggars in search of food to come in, the Pharisee's admirers to listen to the discussion and a woman such as this to observe what was going on.

The woman had undoubtedly heard Jesus speak before and, because of his message, she had decided to change her sinful ways.

When the news of Jesus' visit to the Pharisee's house reached her, by way of gratitude, she could not resist bringing perfume for him.

But the nearness of Jesus so moved her that her tears came first and, forgetting that this was something which a decent woman never did in public, she let her hair down to dry Jesus' feet before pouring the perfume on them.

v 39 *If this man really were a prophet, he would know who this woman is who is touching him; he would know what kind of sinful life she lives.*

The woman's sins were likely to have been of a sexual nature and it was thought that she had been leading a life of prostitution.

To be touched by such a woman, as Jesus had been during the meal, would, in the sight of Simon the Pharisee, make Jesus unclean.

Jesus clearly read such condemnation of himself and of the woman in the eyes of his host.

Jesus, in his reply to Simon, tried to move his concern beyond the worry about a religious law being broken to a much more important one – the spiritual need of the woman.

This is the same point which Jesus had to make in the argument which followed his healing of the crippled woman on the Sabbath.

In order to teach Simon this lesson, Jesus told him a parable about forgiveness. Simon agreed that the debtor with the most debt would love the moneylender most.

Questions on the Commentary

1. What did Zacchaeus do to get a glimpse of Jesus?

2. Why was he taking a risk in doing this?

3. (i) What did Jesus ask of Zacchaeus?

   (ii) Why would Zacchaeus be surprised at Jesus' request?

4. In entering Zacchaeus' home, what was Jesus teaching everyone about God?

5. In groups of six, re-enact this story. Some of the group should be the crowd who give Zacchaeus a hard time when they see him.

6. On the occasion when Jesus had a meal in Levi's house, what did he say to those who accused him of keeping bad company?

7. Using the examples of **three** meetings which Jesus had with people, explain how and why Jesus came into conflict with Pharisees.

CONTEMPORARY ISSUES

1. OUTCASTS

The novel *About a Boy* by Nick Hornby is about a twelve-year-old boy called Marcus who has recently moved house. He is having problems fitting in to his new school. Like Zacchaeus, he is an outcast.

He got to school early, went to the form room, sat down at his desk. He was safe enough there . . . What was there to laugh at? Not much really, unless you were the kind of person who was on permanent lookout for something to laugh at.

Unfortunately, that was the kind of person most kids were, in his experience. They patrolled up and down school corridors like sharks, except that what they were on the look out for wasn't flesh but the wrong trousers, or the wrong hair cut, or the wrong shoes, any or all of which sent them wild with excitement. As he was usually wearing the wrong shoes or the wrong trousers, and his haircut was wrong all the time, every day of the week, he didn't have to do very much to send them all demented.

1. Why is Marcus unhappy at school?

2. Do you agree with Marcus that most kids are on the permanent lookout for something to laugh at?

3. What does he mean by the 'wrong' hair cut etc?

4. How important is it amongst your group of friends to have the 'right' clothes etc?

2. **TWO PIECES OF WRITING ABOUT PREJUDICE**

MEMBERS ONLY

Of course you may join our club
Everybody's welcome.
Er – you are not Jewish by any chance?
I mean, not that we are prejudiced or anything only
When you said your name was Greenberg . . .
What I'm saying is

I have nothing against Catholics you understand.
They are all right in their place,
Rome.
But one has to keep up the standard.
This is an exclusive club.
You don't have to belong to a public school to join.
Not one of the big ones anyway.
But it would be all too easy to lower the tone, then,
The next thing you know they will start
Letting white people in.

The most famous speech by the black American Civil Rights campaigner Martin Luther King is called *I have a Dream*.

I have a dream that one day on the red hills of Georgia the sons of the former slaves and the sons of the former slave owners will be able to sit down together at the table of brotherhood . . . I have a dream that my four little children one day will live in a nation where they will not be judged by the colour of their skin, but by the content of their character.

1. In your own words explain what the word *prejudice* means.

2. Use the poem to make a list of the different kinds of people against whom the person who is speaking has a prejudice.

3. Use the library to find out how Martin Luther King used non-violence as a means of protest.

4. Design a poster to encourage racial tolerance rather than prejudice.

5. *David's first week in the pre-prep*

    David had a wonderful first week at school. He had loved every minute of it. He could not wait for each day and he would be dressed and ready by half past six! As it happened, Friday was the first day of that first week that his mother could pick him up. He could not wait to point out Simon to her, his new friend, whom he had spoken about each evening, nonstop! Neither David nor his mother knew then that Simon was the son of an African diplomat who had recently moved to their neighbourhood.

    Friday came at long last. David was standing by his mother and was anxiously waiting for Simon to emerge from the door. Unlike Simon, David and all the other children were white. David thought long and hard about what he could say that would distinguish Simon from all the others in the group as he came out.

    'There he is, there he is, mummy, there's Simon, see, he's the one with the green jumper.'

    What does this true story tell us about the nature of prejudice?

Common Entrance Questions

1. (a) How did Zacchaeus make sure that he could see Jesus? (1)

   (b) Zacchaeus was a tax-collector. Name another tax-collector who followed Jesus. (1)

   (c) What did Zacchaeus promise to do? (3)

   (d) Explain why tax-collectors were disliked so much. (5)

   (e) Tax-collectors were seen as outcasts. Explain why Pharisees complained so much when Jesus ate with outcasts. (5)

   (f) Zacchaeus was very unpopular. Imagine that you provide answers to problems sent by children to a magazine. Write out your letter of advice to a twelve year old who feels unpopular at school. (10)

2. (a) Where was Levi when Jesus called him? (1)

   (b) What did Jesus say to him? (1)

   (c) Why was Levi regarded as an outcast? (3)

   (d) Describe the events which took place later on that day at Levi's house. (5)

   (e) Explain why Jesus was happy to eat with sinners. (5)

   (f) 'There are no good reasons to help outcasts today.' Do you agree with this statement? Provide full reasons for your answer. (10)

3. (a) A woman who was regarded as an outcast and a sinner washed Jesus' feet. Where was Jesus at the time? (1)

   (b) What did she pour on his feet? (1)

   (c) We are told that Jesus forgave the woman's sins. What was the reaction of the people who saw and heard him do this? (3)

   (d) To illustrate his teaching, Jesus told a parable. Briefly retell this parable. (5)

   (e) Explain what you think this story tells us about Jesus' work. (5)

   (f) Who might today's outcasts be and should we help them all? Give reasons for your answer. (10)

4. (a) What was the name of the Pharisee who entertained Jesus for a meal? (1)

   (b) During the meal a woman stood behind Jesus. What did she do? (2)

   (c) Why was the Pharisee upset by the woman's actions? (2)

   (d) Retell the short parable which Jesus told in answer to the Pharisees' displeasure. (5)

   (e) Explain the meaning of the parable. (5)

   (f) It used to be said that women in our society were not given the same rights and opportunities as men. Do you think this is still true? Give full reasons for your views. (10)

Scholarship Questions

1. (a) Use examples from the New Testament to illustrate Jesus' teaching about outcasts. (8)

   (b) Who do you see as the outcasts today? What might be done to help them become part of society again? (12)

2. 'Wherever different human cultures live together, there prejudice will inevitably be found.' Write your comments in full about this statement. (20)

3. There has been a long history of prejudice against each other in the Protestant and Catholic communities in Northern Ireland. At the height of the troubles in the 1970s a thirteen-year-old girl wrote the following:

   On Monday 12 February, it started to snow. It had snowed all night and in the morning it had settled on the roofs and trees and cars. At morning break, we had a snowball fight with the prefects and the masters. We rolled big Ted, the woodwork master, in the snow. But the best fun of all came at lunchtime. Every day there is a running battle between us Catholics and the Protestants, so the army have to escort us down the road. But that day I saw a very strange thing. Catholics and Protestants, police and soldiers, were all snowballing each other and laughing happily. It was a very strange thing and we all enjoyed it. But I don't think I will see anything like it again.

   Answer the following questions about the above description of the snowball fight.

   (a) Why did the snow change things? (4)

   (b) Why does the girl think it will not happen again? (4)

   (c) Imagine you are a teacher who witnesses these events. Describe what you did the next day in order to build on the fact that children from both sides of the divide laughed together. (12)

4. From what does western society need salvation? (20)

5. Imagine you are Zacchaeus. Write your diary entry for the day before Jesus' visit to your house and the one for the day after. (20)

3

ON BEING A FOLLOWER OF JESUS

THE CALL OF THE DISCIPLES

LUKE 5 vv 1–11

The nets were about to break

SUMMARY OF THE TEXT

While standing on the shore of Lake Gennesaret as people were approaching to listen, Jesus saw fishermen washing their nets.

He got into Simon's boat and asked him to push the boat out a little way from the shore so that he could teach the crowd.

When he had finished speaking, he suggested to Simon that they move to deeper water to fish.

Despite the fact they had been fishing unsuccessfully all night, Simon obeyed Jesus.

When they let down the net, it became so full that it nearly burst, so the other boat came to help them.

Even so, it seemed as though both boats would sink with the weight of fish.

Simon then fell on his knees before Jesus and said, 'Go away from me, Lord! I am a sinful man!'

James and John, the sons of Zebedee, Simon's partners, were also amazed at the large number of fish.

Jesus said to Simon, 'Don't be afraid; from now on you will be catching men.'

Without hesitation Simon, James and John pulled their boats up the beach, left everything and followed him.

COMMENTARY ON THE TEXT

v 1 *Gennesaret* is another name for Lake Galilee.

v 4 *Push the boat out further to the deep water, and you and your partners let down your nets for a catch.*

The men had been up all night fishing without success. They must have been tired, yet they could not resist staying to hear what Jesus had to say to the crowds who stood on the shore of their lake.

Clearly Jesus' words had an impact on them because Simon did not hesitate to take the boat out again on Jesus' command.

v 8 *Go away from me, Lord! I am a sinful man!*

It was not the amazing catch of fish which caused Simon to be aware of his own sin. It was the impact of Jesus' message and his obvious goodness which brought Simon to his knees.

v 10 *Don't be afraid; from now on you will be catching people.*

These fishermen were the sort of men whom Jesus needed as disciples. They were clearly used to hard work which sometimes brought no reward. They were also the sort of men who, once they believed, were willing to obey and to follow Jesus without hesitation.

THE RICH YOUNG MAN

MARK 10 vv 17–22

SUMMARY OF THE TEXT

As Jesus was setting out on a journey, a young man ran up to him and asked Jesus what he must do to inherit eternal life.

Jesus reminded him of some of the Ten Commandments.

The man replied that he had kept all the Commandments. Jesus said that even so, there was one thing more he should do.

He must go and sell all his possessions, give the money raised to the poor, then immediately follow him.

On hearing this, the man's face fell and he went away with a sad heart, because he was wealthy.

COMMENTARY ON THE TEXT

v 17 . . . *a man ran up and knelt before him* . . .

The fact that the man knelt shows that he was sincere in his question. He was not trying to trick Jesus, as was the lawyer who asked him the same question *(see chapter 8)*.

Another sign of his sincerity was to call Jesus 'Good Teacher'. The fact that Jesus invited the young man to follow him shows that Jesus valued the young man's sincerity and enthusiasm.

. . . *What must I do* . . .?

The young man's question comes from thinking that a good relationship with God is based upon keeping enough of the 613 religious laws which the Old Testament offers the Jew for everyday life. These are to be found in the books of *Exodus*, *Leviticus*, *Deuteronomy* and *Numbers*. In the same way, a muscle builder might ask how many press-ups he needed to do to build up his arms, or a prep school pupil might ask how many pluses she needed for the reward of wearing play clothes at the end of term!

. . . to receive eternal life?

The young man was not asking what he must do to go to Heaven. *Eternal life* here means being close to God and part of God's kingdom. This was not, for them, a place they thought they went to after death. The Kingdom of God which Jesus taught about could be entered there and then by anyone who followed his teaching about God.

Jesus taught that anyone who followed his teaching could experience the nearness of God in everyday life and so feel part of his Kingdom.

v 18 Why do you call me good?

Jesus was reminding the young man and those around him that he did not want to appear as important as God. Jesus wanted to point the young man not to himself but to the claims of God.

v 19 You know the commandments . . .

Jesus quotes the last six commandments. These are not in the order in which they appear in *Exodus 20*. Also the Tenth Commandment is slightly changed here. These last six are the commandments which are concerned with human relationships.

v 21 . . . then come and follow me.

This could simply mean follow the teaching of Jesus. However, it is more usually understood as an invitation to be one of the disciples who had left everything they had and, when asked by Jesus, followed him.

v 22 . . . he was very rich.

The call to give everything away would surprise not only the young man, but some of those around him as well. They would think of wealth as a sign of God's favour.

However, there was also another view in some of the *Psalms* (the religious poetry of the Old Testament). Here the poor are linked with those who pray to God regularly and the rich with those who ignore Him. Jesus' whole teaching is concerned with reminding everyone that there is no richer human experience than choosing God's Kingdom. Elsewhere Jesus likens this putting the Kingdom of God before all else in life to a man selling everything so that he can buy a 'pearl of great price'. For Jesus, this pearl of great price is the Kingdom of God.

CONTEMPORARY ISSUES

WEALTH AND HAPPINESS

(i) A member of the House of Lords said in a newspaper interview that his seven-year-old granddaughter considered a designer label on her jeans to be so important that she would refuse to wear jeans from Marks and Spencer.

1. Why does the little girl think in this way about her jeans?

2. In which ways do we judge people by what they wear rather than what they are?

(ii) In a discussion group of thirteen year olds, David said this about a boy who was having problems fitting in.

Barry has everything, yet in another way he has nothing. He lives in an enormous house. He goes sailing practically every weekend. He has all the latest football strips – home and away – and the England tops, but he is the most unpopular boy in the year. I remember when we were 7, I had been invited for the day. I went to his room. It was like Toys R Us. I picked up one of the Game Boys and he immediately told me to put it down. It was the same all day. I couldn't touch anything without him sounding off at me. He spent the whole time showing off. He said that he was the best bowler, had scored the most goals for the village team. It's rubbish. I saw him in games. He is always last to be picked because he is so hopeless and no one likes him. I couldn't wait for my mum to pick me up. It was just me and him, yet he wouldn't share anything. Do you know – he is still the same. He hasn't changed and now he's 13!

1. In which ways did Barry have everything and yet have nothing?

2. Which important truth did David share with the group in his story about when he and Barry were seven?

3. What big mistakes in relationships did Barry make?

4. Imagine that, after hearing David, you and some others decide to try to help Barry. Outline a plan of action with suggestions which you might try.

5. Discuss the question 'Will Barry ever change?'

Design a poster with the title 'The Kingdom of Heaven'.

Common Entrance Questions

1. (a) In which lake did Jesus help the men who were to become his disciples catch 'such a large number of fish that their nets were about to break'? (1)

   (b) What did Simon Peter do when Jesus told him to push the boat out and let down the nets for a catch? (2)

   (c) What was Simon Peter's reaction after the fish had been caught, and what did he say? (2)

   (d) When Jesus called a rich young man to follow him, what was he told to do and how did the story end? (5)

   (e) Explain why you think **either** Simon Peter **or** the rich young man reacted in the way he did. Give your reasons. (5)

   (f) Write about someone, not from the Bible, who has been prepared to give up everything for a cause which he/she believed to be right. Explain why you think that he/she acted in this way. (10)

2. (a) Who said to Jesus, 'Good Master, what must I do to receive eternal life?' (1)

   (b) What question did Jesus immediately ask him in return? (2)

   (c) What, eventually, did Jesus ask him to do? (2)

   (d) Why do you think both Jesus and the man were sad at the end of their meeting? (5)

   (e) What do you think the man had expected Jesus to say? (5)

   (f) Is it possible to be wealthy and a follower of Jesus? Explain what the difficulties might be. (10)

3. (a) *Go and sell everything you have and give the money to the poor.*

   (i) Describe how Jesus came to say these words to a young man. (10)

   (ii) Explain what you think the young man expected Jesus to say to him. (5)

   (b) Describe the work of any charity supported by you, your family or the school. Your answer should not be about how funds have been raised, but rather, who benefits from the money and in which ways they benefit. (10)

Scholarship Questions

1. From what you know about what Jesus said to the rich young man, what do you think his message would be to the rich of today's world? (20)

2. Both a lawyer and a rich young man asked Jesus the same question.

    (a) What was the question? (5)

    (b) What do you think was different about Jesus' attitude to each questioner? (5)

    (c) What do you think the *Kingdom of God* means for the world today? (10)

3. Does wealth have to get in the way of a religious life? (20)

4. What do you think it means to be a follower of Jesus today? Give your reasons. (20)

THE REQUEST OF JAMES AND JOHN

MARK 10 vv 35–45

SUMMARY OF THE TEXT

James and John, two of Jesus' disciples, asked him if, when the Kingdom came, they could sit in the most important seats, that is, on Jesus' right and left.

Jesus then explained to them that being a disciple of his would mean that they would experience suffering.

The other disciples were annoyed with them for asking this question.

Jesus gave them further teaching and explained that, among his followers, whoever wished to be great must be the servant of all, just as he had come to serve and offer his life on behalf of everyone else.

COMMENTARY ON THE TEXT

v 35 . . . *James and John, the sons of Zebedee . . .*

In *St Matthew's Gospel*, it was the mother of James and John who made the request to Jesus *(Matthew 20 vv 20–28)*. Perhaps this was because Matthew was too embarrassed to write that the disciples themselves had made such a selfish request. Such thoughts were completely the opposite of all that Jesus taught about greatness. The last thing he was concerned about was worldly position and status.

It is possible that James and John were thinking that Jesus was on the way to Jerusalem to seize the throne of David and be the Messiah the crowds wanted. If so, there would be a real throne to sit either side of!

Right hand and left are positions of honour at a formal dinner. James and John think of the future only in terms of glory for themselves. Little do they know that to be at Jesus' right and left was to be the fate of the two thieves who were crucified with him.

v 38 . . . *the cup* . . .

This is a metaphor. It is used in the Old Testament to mean whatever God has in store

138

for a person. Jesus has to teach them that the *cup* which they will share with him is one of suffering and death.

Baptised in this verse comes from the Greek word meaning *to be flooded with calamities.*

In answer to the question from Jesus, James and John said: 'We can', which shows that they did not understand what Jesus was saying. James was to be put to death by Herod at an early date *(Acts 12 v 2)* but the fate of John is not certain. One source has him martyred, but according to another he lived to a ripe old age in Ephesus.

v 41 . . . *the other ten disciples* . . . *became angry with James and John.*

This was not necessarily because they understood the teaching of Jesus any better. They may have been angry because James and John got in with the question first!

A Messiah who is a 'suffering servant'

v 45 For even the Son of Man did not come to be served; he came to serve and to give his life to redeem many people.

Jesus acted out the first part of this verse, just before his death, by washing the disciples' feet, the lowliest job of a house servant. Among Jesus' followers true greatness can only be shown by humility.

Here also we are provided with a clue to the sort of Messiah which Jesus saw himself to be: one who served and one who suffered for the sake of others. Many believe that this idea came from reading the Old Testament book of the prophet *Isaiah chapter 53 v 11*:

> *My devoted servant, with whom I am well pleased, will bear the punishment of many and for his sake I will forgive them.*

A *redemption* was the money paid for setting free a slave. Jesus' followers came to believe that Jesus' death on the cross was an act of redemption, a setting free of mankind from the slavery of sin.

By following Jesus, man obtains the wholehearted generous forgiveness of God (as that shown by the father in the *Parable of the Lost Son*). Jews would also see the parallel between Moses and Jesus. God used Moses to set the people free from slavery in Egypt. God used Jesus, His Messiah, to set the people free from their sins. Through Jesus they were redeemed.

Questions on the Commentary

1. Why did James and John ask for what they did?

2. Why does Matthew write this story with the mother of James and John making this request?

3. What did being at the right and left hand of Jesus come to mean later on in the story of his life?

4. In the Bible what is *cup* a metaphor for?

5. Where in the Bible did the idea of the Messiah as a suffering servant come from?

6. What does the word *redemption* mean?

7. In trying to understand the meaning of Jesus' life and death, which parallel did his followers see in the life of Moses?

CONTEMPORARY ISSUES

TRUE GREATNESS

(i) **My first camp**

When I was eleven I went to camp for the first time. It was at Prestatyn in North Wales. I belonged to a uniformed organisation called 'The Church Lads' Brigade' (CLB). I joined because I liked the uniform. I soon came to realise that the adult leaders had joined for the same reason. Their uniform was wonderful too – almost identical to that of an army officer – complete with a Sam Browne belt and a cane. Even better, we all had ranks, just like the army. I was soon a corporal, longing to be a sergeant, and our leader, who in his daily work was an office cleaner, became on Thursday nights, CLB night, a captain.

At the annual camp they even took the army thing as far as eating separately. There was the officers' mess, the sergeants' mess and the lads' mess.

I can't remember much about any of the captains, the majors or the colonel. I can only remember Bill. He didn't eat anywhere special because he cooked for us all. The other job he did was to clean out the lavs or the 'bogs' as we used to call them. He took some getting to know. He never boasted about anything. It was obvious he was qualified in first aid because he dealt with all injuries and ailments as well as everything else. He just got on with things and worked from early morning until late at night. It was only long after he had died and we had all grown up that I realised how important he was to us all and how much 'greater' he was than all of us who 'loved' our uniforms!

1. Why did the grown-ups like the uniform too?

2. Apart from the uniform, how else did the CLB copy the army way of life?

3. Why do you think the grown-up telling this story remembers Bill most, whilst the others were forgotten?

(ii) **Flo saves the day**

St Anne's Church in Liverpool provided a house in which those who had come out of mental hospital could stay for a short while before going home. They called it 'Open Circle'. Two of the residents, Lilly and Barbara, had agreed to help at the church jumble sale which was in aid of funds for the Open Circle.

This task was difficult for Lilly and Barbara because they were recovering from agoraphobia, an illness which made them afraid of going out of the house. Eventually, they felt brave enough to go, as they had promised. Their job was to make the tea. As there was no one in the kitchen, they began to help themselves to tea and sugar from the cupboards.

'Who told you you could have those? The sugar is the nursery group's, the tea is the men's club. Put them back at once!'

It was the bossy voice of the church hall caretaker, Nellie Heckle, a leading member of the church. Lilly and Barbara were just about to grab their coats again in panic and head home when the day was saved.

'Hello. Can you help me?' said a much kinder voice. 'My name's Flo Marsh – I haven't done this before. Can you show me what to do?'

Lilly and Barbara explained what had happened and together, with their confidence returned, thanks to Flo, they set about their tea-making and had a very happy afternoon raising money for Open Circle, St Anne's mental health project.

141

The strange thing was that of all the people there that day, Flo was one of the most capable. She was the district nurse.

---

1. What project had St Anne's church set up for the mentally ill?

2. What illness did Lilly and Barbara suffer from and how did it affect them?

3. Which surprising piece of information do we discover about

   (a) Nellie Heckle

   (b) Flo Marsh?

4. Explain how Flo saved the day.

5. Why do you think St Anne's set up the Open Circle? Would you expect the church to be involved in this kind of project?

(iii) **David Hughes**

Dave Hughes would never be famous for his high marks. The girls in his year would say that he would be famous for his smile and his eyes, and the boys for his sporting skills.

He was gifted enough to be good at all sports. By the time he reached the top of the school at 13, he was captain of everything. No one grumbled because, not only was he the best player in every sport, he was also the most humble boy in the year. Everyone felt comfortable with him. He would muck about with the 10 year olds at break time and play at their level, never showing off. He never boasted about his runs, his tries or his goals.

What I remember most about him was his rugby. He was one of those players who you knew, once he had collected the ball at speed, no one could catch him. It was breathtaking to see him so certainly heading for the line. Yet often in the second half, when the match was obviously ours, I have seen him pass the ball just before the line to someone who had never scored, to let them have the glory. Some captain!

---

1. What do you think was the secret of David's popularity?

2. What do you think he did that made him special?

3. What have extracts (i), (ii) and (iii) got in common?

Common Entrance Questions

1. (a)   Who was the father of James and John?   (1)

    (b)   What did James and John ask of Jesus?   (2)

    (c)   Why were the other disciples angry with them?   (2)

    (d)   'If one of you wants to be great, he must be the servant of the rest.'
          What do you think Jesus meant by these words?   (5)

    (e)   Why did Jesus teach that it would be very difficult to follow him?   (5)

    (f)   'Everyone can be great. Because everybody can serve.' Write about
          someone who has worked in the service of others.   (10)

2. *If one of you wants to be great, he must be the servant of the rest.*
    (Mark 10 v 43)

    (a)   What question prompted Jesus to say these words?   (5)

    (b)   What other teaching did Jesus give in reply to the question?   (10)

    (c)   Describe someone you would regard as *great* and explain why.   (10)

3. *Can you drink the cup of suffering I must drink?* (Mark 10 v 38)

    (a)   What does the word *cup* mean in this verse?   (5)

    (b)   Explain in detail what Jesus was teaching the disciples in this
          passage.   (10)

    (c)   Describe the life of anyone you know who has suffered for his/her faith. (10)

Scholarship Questions

1. (a) Which question did James and John ask Jesus? (4)

   (b) Why do you think this story has been changed in *St Matthew's Gospel* where the question is put by their mother? (4)

   (c) Outline the qualities which, in your opinion, make someone great. (12)

2. Use your knowledge of the *Gospels* to describe what Jesus expected from his followers. (20)

3. Describe a life worth living. (20)

4

MIRACLES OF HEALING

THE PARALYSED MAN

MARK 2 vv 1–12

they let the man down, lying on his mat (Mark 2 v 4)

SUMMARY OF THE TEXT

When Jesus returned to Capernaum, the house in which he was teaching became so full that even the front door was blocked with a crowd.

Four men arrived, carrying a paralysed man.

When they could not get in, they broke through the roof and lowered the man down into the house on a mat.

When Jesus saw their faith, he forgave the man his sins.

Some teachers of the Law who were present expressed outrage and accused Jesus of blasphemy because, in their view, only God could forgive sins. Jesus knew what they were thinking and asked whether it was easier to say the words of forgiveness or to ask the man to get up.

So in order to prove that he did indeed have the authority to forgive sins, Jesus then invited the paralysed man to get up.

This the man did, much to everyone's amazement.

COMMENTARY ON THE TEXT

This is another story in which religious leaders argued with Jesus. Mark shows that they did not recognise him as God's Messiah. They did not realise that Jesus did in fact have the authority to forgive sins because he was the Messiah.

v 4 So they made a hole in the roof.

It would have been relatively simple for the men to break up the mixture of twigs, matting and earth which filled the space between the beams of the roof, although clearly some debris would have fallen on the heads of those below!

v 5 Seeing how much faith they had . . .

Jesus was moved by the faith of the four friends as well as that of the paralysed man. But Jesus' response to their faith was at first surprising. Instead of the expected words of healing, he spoke words of forgiveness. This came from the ancient world view that disease was a result of previous sins.

v 6 Some teachers of the Law who were sitting there . . .

The teachers of the law would be horrified at Jesus' saying words of forgiveness to the paralysed man. To begin with, the religious law demanded much ritual washing to get rid of sin, in order for it to be forgiven. Words alone would not do. Furthermore, the power to forgive sin belonged only to God and not to humans. So, in their eyes, Jesus was guilty of blasphemy – an offence against God. It was to be for crimes of blasphemy that these religious leaders put Jesus on trial for his life.

v 9 Is it easier to say . . . 'Your sins are forgiven . . . '?

In the ancient world it was commonly believed that disease or handicap came as result

146

of sin. It was therefore part of the healing process, in this case, to forgive the man's sins.

v 10 *I will prove to you, then, that the Son of Man has authority on earth to forgive sins.*

Son of Man is the title which Jesus most often used of himself. It is quite likely that, when he used this name for himself, he was thinking of the Old Testament book of *Daniel*. In *Daniel chapter 7* there is the vision of the Son of Man in the clouds. There, the *Good News Bible* translates *Son of Man* as *human being*.

In *Daniel 7 v 14* this heavenly person is given *authority, honour and royal power* from the *one who has been living for ever.*

In order then to prove the authority he had from God, Jesus healed the paralysed man.

This is very typical of the miracle stories of the *Gospels*. They are not meant to be magical acts (as jumping off the pinnacle of the temple would have been). Jesus' work of healing is always presented as a sign of the Kingdom of God or of Jesus' own authority.

Also, the healing miracles are usually brought about because of the faith of the victim, or of a friend or relative of the sick person.

Questions on the Commentary

1. What evidence is there in the text about the quality of the friendship which the paralysed man enjoyed?

2. What moved Jesus to heal the paralysed man and why did he speak words of forgiveness first?

3. Why did these words of Jesus cause outrage amongst the teachers of the Law?

4. What did Jesus mean when he spoke of himself as *Son of Man*?

5. Imagine that you are a journalist following Jesus. Produce an article under one of the following headlines:

   (i)   Another Clash with Authority for Jesus

   (ii) Four Friends Find a Way

CONTEMPORARY ISSUES

1. FRIENDSHIP

(i)   In a class of Indian children from the very north of Canada, if one of them gets an answer, he shares it with the others, then they all put their hands up at once. The one with the answer would not dream of taking the credit alone. To do so would make him gain a small reward at the cost of the community of his friends.

1. Explain what is different between this class and yours.

2. What are the advantages and disadvantages of working like this as a group?

3. What do you think the relationships between this class will be like outside lessons?

(ii)   Work in groups of six.

1. Each member should first write down in order the **four** most important ingredients of lasting friendship. Then as a group share your ideas and vote for which four are the most important.

2. Make a list of the things that you have faith in. Each member shares that list with the others to find whether there are any big similarities or big differences.

(iii) You are the school counsellor. Write a reply to the following letter which has been sent to you.

Dear Counsellor,

Please give me advice. Millie is my best friend but she doesn't save a place for me every lesson and she doesn't want to hang around with me every break-time. I get really jealous when I see her going off with other people. I think that she has told some people my secrets. We promised each other that we wouldn't tell anyone else. She says I am moody. I had a row with Rachael last week, so I told the rest of my friends not to speak to her as well. But Millie is still speaking to her. Some friend! The trouble is I still really like Millie but I think we are drifting apart. What should I do?

2. FAITH HEALING TODAY

In the late 1970s a chaplain from Sevenoaks School in Kent wrote a letter to *The Times*. In it he explained that he had taken his sixth form RS group on an outing to watch a faith healer at work. Much to his surprise, a boy in his group, who had broken his leg in a skiing accident, discovered that it had been cured.

1. Why do you think the school chaplain bothered to write about this to *The Times*?

2. Do you think that this event proves anything about religion?

3. Why do you think that the boy's leg was cured?

Common Entrance Questions

1. (a)   Who brought a paralysed man to be healed by Jesus?   (1)

    (b)   What did Jesus say to the paralysed man?   (2)

    (c)   Who disapproved of what Jesus said and of what offence did they accuse him?   (2)

    (d)   Briefly describe what happened immediately after Jesus had healed a crippled woman on the Sabbath.   (5)

    (e)   Explain what you think these two miracle stories tell us about Jesus.   (5)

    (f)   Faith is often shown as being very important in the story of Jesus. Write an account of the life of someone of great faith in the last century.   (10)

2. (a)   In which village was the paralysed man healed?   (1)

    (b)   Why could the friends not get the man through the door?   (2)

    (c)   How did they eventually get the paralysed man to meet Jesus?   (2)

    (d)   Describe how Jesus' healing of this man caused an argument.   (5)

    (e)   Explain the meaning of Jesus' answer to those who argued with him.   (5)

    (f)   Should we expect miracles to happen today? Give reasons for your answer.   (10)

3. *I will prove to you then that the Son of Man has authority on earth to forgive sins.* (Mark 2 v 10)

    (a)   Who is the *Son of Man*?   (1)

    (b)   On which occasion did Jesus say these words?   (2)

    (c)   What did Jesus do next in the story?   (2)

    (d)   Explain why an argument occurred between Jesus and the authorities.   (5)

    (e)   What caused another argument when Jesus healed a crippled woman?   (5)

    (f)   What actions do you think can never be forgiven? Explain fully.   (10)

4. *So they made a hole in the roof right above the place where Jesus was.* (Mark 2 v 4)

   (a) Who are the *they* in this verse? (1)

   (b) Where did these events take place? (1)

   (c) What did Jesus say when he realised what they had done? (3)

   (d) Why did Jesus' words cause offence? (5)

   (e) Explain which reasons Jesus gave for his actions after he answered his accusers. (5)

   (f) What difficulties do today's religious leaders face when they claim to be acting in God's name? Give a full answer. (10)

Scholarship Questions

1. *I will prove to you then that the Son of Man has authority on earth to forgive sins.*

   (a) What do you understand by the title *Son of Man*? (3)

   (b) Describe fully the events immediately before and after Jesus said these words. (7)

   (c) With the support of other examples, explain why controversy often accompanied Jesus' words and actions. (10)

2. 'Faith can move mountains.' Write in full your opinions about this claim. (20)

3. (a) 'Get up, pick up your mat and go home!' Describe, in full, the occasion when Jesus said this. (8)

   (b) 'I don't know what I have done to deserve this.' This phrase is still uttered today at times of suffering and bereavement. Explain fully what belief lies behind this statement and express your views about this belief in detail. (12)

JESUS HEALS A CRIPPLED WOMAN ON THE SABBATH

LUKE 13 vv 10–17

SUMMARY OF THE TEXT

Jesus was teaching in a synagogue on the Sabbath when he laid his hands upon a woman to cure her from a crippling disease.

She had suffered from it for eighteen years.

Immediately, an official of the synagogue protested that Jesus had broken the Sabbath law.

Jesus accused him, and those like him, of hypocrisy.

If they had an ox, they would certainly water it, Sabbath day or not!

How much more then should this woman be helped on the Sabbath.

When they heard this, his enemies felt ashamed.

COMMENTARY ON THE TEXT

v 14 *The official of the synagogue . . .*

Today the synagogue remains the place of worship for Jews who gather there on Friday evenings to hear readings from the Bible at the start of the Sabbath day. (Remember, Jewish days start at sunset, so the Saturday Sabbath starts at sunset on Friday.)

At the time of Jesus, there were several important religious leaders of the Jewish people. As we have seen, the *Gospels* often present Jesus' words or actions as giving offence to these officials.

Some of the other important religious leaders whom he encountered besides this one were the Pharisees, the Sadducees and the Lawyers.

Pharisees

These men were experts on the Law contained in the Old Testament books of *Exodus*, *Leviticus*, *Numbers* and *Deuteronomy*. These books contain 613 commandments (rules) about everyday life which an orthodox (strict) Jew should observe.

Often, the Pharisees were scribes as well. This meant they had learned the art of reading and writing Hebrew. They would be able to make new copies of the Bible.

They would not only know every detail of the Law, but give advice about how it should be acted upon.

Sadducees

This was a group of men who, again, knew the Bible thoroughly, but who had different opinions on certain religious issues, such as not believing in life after death.

Lawyers

These men were not lawyers as we would recognise the term. They were not involved with the laws of the land. Like Pharisees, they were experts on the religious law as set down in the Bible.

In a society which was occupied by Rome, and in which people from other cultures traded, these religious leaders had to police the beliefs of their people. They acted as 'thought police' to stop the people drifting into slack observance of the Law, as the Samaritans had done.

The Law as an obstacle

This story of the crippled woman provides a typical example of the upset Jesus gave to the religious leaders. As a Jew, Jesus of course would also believe that the Law of God must be loved, respected and valued as His precious gift to His people. The problem as Jesus saw it was that the religious leaders of his day were so absorbed in the detail of the Law that they could not see when a strict keeping of the Law got in the way of doing what was obviously right!

In the case of this woman, Jesus thought it was especially appropriate that it was on the Sabbath day that he was setting her free from the burden of a crippling disease. For the Sabbath was the one day of the week, when the Jews, when they were in captivity in Egypt, had been free from the burden of slavery.

The purpose of Jesus' miracles

Jesus' miracles were not only about caring for others. His teaching often pointed to the nearness of the Kingdom of God. By recording these miracles, the Gospel writers also wanted to show the nearness of God's Kingdom in Jesus' **actions** as well as his **words**.

Questions on the Commentary

1. What do you understand by the word *synagogue*?

2. Why do Jews congregate for worship on a Friday evening if their Sabbath is Saturday?

3. Write what you know about the following religious leaders at the time of Jesus:

   (i) Pharisees

   (ii) lawyers.

4. Imagine that you are a Pharisee at the time of Jesus. Write a report on him for your superiors who have heard that he attracts crowds with his talk of God's Kingdom and his supposed miracles.

5. What was Jesus' view about the criticisms made by the official of the synagogue?

CONTEMPORARY ISSUES

1. RULES FOR LIVING IN A COMMUNITY

(i) Some schools produce a large booklet of school rules. Others do not. If you were head of a school, would you think it necessary to produce such a booklet? Present both sides of the argument, as well as your own view.

(ii)   Imagine that members of your form are the only survivors of a plane crash and you find yourself without any adults. Your form mates look to you for ideas. You call a meeting and provide some suggestions about how you will live together successfully until you are rescued. Write down what you will say to them.

2. ST TARDIS – A CHURCH FOR HANDICAPPED CHILDREN

In the 1970s the church of St James Clapton, in the East End of London, was hidden between a sex cinema and a frozen-food store. The cinema notice board advertised films such as 'Nudes of the World' alongside the church wall. It looked very odd! The church was huge and largely empty on Sundays.

A small group who worshipped in the church decided they should make better use of this vast building and share it with anyone who could make use of the church in the week. And that is exactly what happened.

They were awarded grants of money to convert the nave of the church into a three-storey centre for handicapped children and their families who desperately needed space to meet and to play. The then Bishop of Stepney, Trevor Huddleston, loved children and did all he could to help the plans become a reality.

The building is now a great success. The ground floor of the centre has a small swimming-pool. The middle floor has a workshop so that toys can be made for the children. The top floor is a large open space for meetings and games. At one end is the lovely big rose window of the church. The church people now meet in the sanctuary which has been decorated and is much easier to heat in winter. But, best of all, each day the Huddleston Centre is full of handicapped children enjoying the lovely environment which has been created for them.

Some people call the church 'St Tardis' because Dr Who's Tardis looked like a police box on the outside but was something else on the inside. St James Clapton also looks rather ordinary and unpromising on the outside; inside there is a wonderful and unexpected transformation of space.

1. What was odd about where St James' was?

2. Why did the church people decide to share their church?

3. With whom did they share it?

4. Describe what was actually built.

5. Prepare a talk on the life of Trevor Huddleston and find out what he was even more famous for.

1. (a) Jesus healed a crippled woman on the Sabbath. How had she been affected by the illness? (1)

    (b) What had caused the crippled woman's illness? (2)

    (c) What did Jesus say to the woman? (2)

    (d) Outline the discussion which followed between Jesus and the official of the synagogue. (5)

    (e) Explain the importance of faith in the healing miracles of Jesus. (5)

    (f) 'The word miracle has been over used and does not mean anything today.' Do you agree? Give reasons for your answer. (10)

2. (a) For how long had the woman been crippled before Jesus healed her in the synagogue? (1)

    (b) What did the woman do when Jesus placed his hands on her? (2)

    (c) Why was the official of the synagogue angry when Jesus healed her? (2)

    (d) Describe how Jesus defended his actions. (5)

    (e) Explain what the stories of Jesus' healing miracles tell us about him and his work. (5)

    (f) 'Miracles do not happen today.' Discuss this view. Give full reasoning in your answer. (10)

Scholarship Questions

1. The Gospel stories often tell of confrontations between Jesus and the religious leaders of his day. Write about this from their point of view, giving as many examples as you can. (20)

2. Jesus once accused an official of the synagogue of being a hypocrite. Do you think he would say the same of today's religious leaders? Give your opinion in full. (20)

3. (a) Explain why Jesus was criticised when he healed a crippled woman on the Sabbath, and give details of Jesus' answer to the criticism. (8)

   (b) What do you understand the word *miracle* to mean? (12)

4. Do you think that people today can be healed by faith? Argue your opinion fully. (20)

5

WHO WAS JESUS?

PETER'S DECLARATION

MARK 8 vv 27–33

SUMMARY OF THE TEXT

Jesus asked his disciples the question: 'Who do people say that I am?'

They answered, 'Elijah, John the Baptist or one of the prophets.'

He then asked his disciples, 'Who do you say that I am?'

Peter replied that Jesus was *The Messiah*.

Jesus then told him to keep this secret.

He then went on to tell them that not only must he suffer and be rejected, but that he would be put to death and after three days he would rise again.

Peter was angry with Jesus for speaking about suffering and death, but Jesus rebuked him and continued with his teaching.

Jesus said that those who wanted to follow him must be prepared to take up their cross and face death, as he was about to do.

COMMENTARY ON THE TEXT

This passage is at the heart of what the *Gospel of Mark* is about. It is the turning point of the *Gospel*. From the moment Peter recognised that Jesus was the Messiah, the Christ, Jesus then began the journey from Galilee down to Jerusalem for his arrest, his trial and his death.

Mark was anxious to show what sort of Messiah Jesus was: not a warrior king to lead a revolt against the Romans but a Messiah with a completely different aim.

The fact that not everyone recognised Jesus as the Messiah is again proof that faith was necessary for people to come to this truth. In the creation story, God created humans with the freedom to reject Him. We were not given a 'behaviour chip' in our brains so that, like robots, we would always do what God wanted us to do.

v 28 *Some say that you are John the Baptist, . . . others say that you are Elijah . . .*

The suggestion here is that Jesus is one of the prophets raised from the dead. There is also a belief among Jews that Elijah will appear again just before the Messiah comes. So perhaps that is why some of them thought he was Elijah: he had come as a herald to the Messiah.

v 29 *Peter answered, 'You are the Messiah.'*

This is the conclusion which Mark wanted all those who read his *Gospel* to reach. He wanted his readers, like Peter, to believe this of Jesus.

v 30 *Then Jesus ordered them, 'Do not tell anyone about me.'*

One of the big questions which all the Gospel writers had to face after Jesus had died was this: If Jesus were the Messiah, how was it then that so few people realised it and, worse, he ended up executed as a common criminal on a Roman cross? Some Messiah!

Part of Mark's answer to this problem is given in this verse. Jesus deliberately wanted to keep his identity secret. It was only to be revealed to those who came to the truth of his identity by faith and who then became his followers.

This is why Jesus did not give in to his third temptation, to leap off the pinnacle of the Temple. Jesus wanted people to believe in him by faith, not any other way.

The way of the cross

From this point on in *Mark's Gospel*, the main theme is that of the cross which Jesus will face and how his disciples (not just the Twelve but anyone who wished to follow him) must, like Jesus, be prepared to take up his own cross.

v 32 *He made this very clear to them.*

Whereas Jesus spoke in parables to the crowds, he told his disciples frankly what was to happen to him and what would happen to them if they carried on following him. Jesus realised that his followers would receive the same punishment as himself. Anyone who followed him was likely to be persecuted.

v 36 *Do people gain anything if they win the whole world but lose their life? Of course not!*

These words are quite famous. They turn up in literature or as a saying quoted from the *King James' Version* of the Bible (which was written in the seventeenth century) in this form:

For what shall it profit a man if he gain the whole world, and lose his own soul?

In these words Jesus is again pointing to his core teaching, that the most important aims in human life are not concerned with this world. *Life* in this verse means being part of the Kingdom of God.

v 38 *. . . then the Son of Man will be ashamed of him . . .*

The Son of Man is the title which Jesus most readily uses of himself. This title is linked especially with the coming of God's Kingdom. In the Old Testament book of *Daniel*, the Son of Man appeared riding a chariot in the clouds just before God's Kingdom came.

For a Jew, if things began to go wrong in life, this was a sign that God had removed his favour and was a source, therefore, of shame.

Questions on the Commentary

1. Why is this passage important in *Mark's Gospel*?

2. Why would some of the people think that Jesus was Elijah?

3. Why did Jesus want to keep his Messiahship secret?

4. What meaning did the Jews of Jesus' time give to the word *shame*?

THE TRANSFIGURATION

MARK 9 vv 2–13

SUMMARY OF THE TEXT

Jesus took Peter, James and John up a high mountain.

A change came over Jesus as his clothes became a brilliant shining white.

The three disciples saw Moses and Elijah conversing with Jesus.

Peter suggested that he build shelters for Jesus and the visitors.

He and the others were afraid because of what was happening.

Then a cloud covered them and a voice from the cloud said, 'This is my own dear Son – listen to him!'

Then Jesus was alone and he ordered Peter, James and John not to speak of what they had seen until 'The Son of Man has risen from death'.

They obeyed his order but wondered what Jesus meant by *rising from death*.

They also discussed the reasons for Elijah's presence.

COMMENTARY ON THE TEXT

To Jesus' question at Caesarea Philippi, Peter answered, 'You are the Christ.'

This truth was now confirmed by the story of Jesus' Transfiguration on the mountain top.

Jesus' earthly body was transfigured for a moment into his heavenly body. Jesus was seen in *glory*.

162

v 2 *a high mountain*

The site of the Transfiguration is thought to be Mount Tabor which is not high!

God met Moses on the top of mount Sinai, so the mountain of the Transfiguration is thought of as the new Sinai.

God revealed his name to Moses on Sinai; now on this mountain he revealed Jesus as his only Son.

v 3 *. . . whiter than anyone in the world could wash them.*

This is to make clear that what was happening to Jesus was supernatural – it was of God's doing, not man's.

v 4 *. . . Elijah and Moses . . .*

At the time of Jesus, Jews believed that the great Old Testament figures would appear at the end of this world and play a part in the events leading up to the end. Moses represented Jewish Law and Elijah represented the Prophets.

It is unusual for Elijah to be mentioned before Moses. For Jews, Moses, as the giver of the Law, is regarded as more important. Elijah was probably put first because of his role as the herald of the Messiah.

Both, however, are here with Jesus on the mountain top as witnesses of Jesus' true identity.

v 5 *Peter . . . said . . . we will make three tents . . .* (formerly translated as *tabernacles*).

These would be of the kind made out of plaited branches used in the fields at harvest time. In the Jewish festival of Tabernacles they became reminders of the tents in which the people of Israel lived during their wanderings in the wilderness.

Eventually the belief arose that when the Messiah came, people would again live in tents and God would live with his people as He had done in the past.

This is another good example of Peter being impetuous.

His mistake was to think that the new age could happen without the suffering which Jesus must first undergo.

v 7 *This is my own dear Son – listen to him.*

A voice from the cloud set Jesus apart from Elijah and Moses as being unique. Jesus was God's own Son – his *only* Son, to whom people should now listen.

v 9 *Don't tell anyone about what you have seen until the Son of Man has risen from death.*

This is another example of what is called the *Messianic secret*. If the crowd did not know Jesus was the Messiah, it helps to explain why in the end they rejected him.

We know also that Jesus wanted people to come to him by faith, as Peter had done.

Note that this particular 'secret' was given to just three of the disciples, not the others.

Son of Man is the title which Jesus used most about himself. In the Old Testament book of *Daniel, chapter 7 v 13* the son of man was a heavenly figure, riding a chariot in the clouds to herald the end of time and the coming of God's Kingdom.

v 13 *. . . Elijah has already come . . .*

Jewish teachers believed that Elijah would come as a herald before the appearance of the Messiah. Jesus is here referring to John the Baptist as the herald of his own ministry.

Questions on the Commentary

1. Why is the mountain of the Transfiguration thought of as the new Sinai?

2. What is unusual about the order of the prophets' names in verse 4 of the story?

3. What do Elijah and Moses represent in this story?

4. Why did Peter suggest building tents for Jesus and the two prophets?

5. Why was Peter mistaken in this suggestion?

6. What do you understand by the phrase *Messianic secret*?

CONTEMPORARY ISSUES

1. THE PRICE OF FAME

Jesus attracted large crowds. It is not surprising that he was interested in what people thought about him. He was anxious that they did not look to him for what he was not. Then, as now, it was all too easy to raise false hopes just because of fame.

One *Gospel* story describes how Jesus fed five thousand people who had turned up to see him and hear him speak. Today, we would call Jesus a celebrity. He would receive a lot of media coverage. His private life would be investigated and as many stories as possible would be written about him.

In his own time, Jesus' fame certainly got him into trouble and eventually he was put to death because of what he had said and what he had done.

2. THE COST OF BEING A CELEBRITY TODAY

Are we in danger of doing something of the same with celebrities today? When the Princess of Wales died in a car crash in 1997, the first reports of the crash said that it had happened because her driver was trying to escape the photographers who always followed her.

What right do celebrities have to privacy? To what extent should they be expected to lead morally good lives? How far should we expect celebrities to provide good examples for today's young?

The media today thrives on stories about the lives of film and pop stars, politicians, sporting heroes and members of the royal family. Such people have thousands of words written about them each week. The more sensational the story about them, the more newspapers will be sold and viewing figures will increase.

News reporters are always on the lookout for moral failings in those who have become celebrities.

1. Imagine that Jesus were alive today. Produce a list of **ten** questions which you would ask him if you were interviewing him for a modern chat show.

2. Who are today's heroes? Whom can the young look up to for a good example of how to live?

3. A football star once made a video about how to carry out fouls without being caught by the referee.

   (i) Do you think that such a video should have been made? Give full reasons for your answer.

   (ii) Is it right for us to expect our sporting stars to set a good example to the young, on and off the field?

Common Entrance Questions

1. (a) Which question did Jesus ask his disciples at Caesarea Philippi? (1)

   (b) What was their first answer? (2)

   (c) What was Peter's answer? (2)

   (d) Why did Jesus respond in the way he did to what Peter said? (5)

   (e) What do the Gospel writers want us to learn about Jesus from this story? Give examples and reasons. (5)

   (f) It has been said that if Jesus were to come today, nobody would take any notice. Do you agree with this opinion? Give reasons and defend your view. (10)

2. (a) At Caesarea Philippi, who declared Jesus to be the Messiah? (1)

   (b) What did the title *Messiah* mean for the people in Jesus' time? (2)

   (c) What did Jesus then immediately say? (2)

   (d) What did Jesus then say about suffering? (5)

   (e) Explain what kind of Messiah Jesus was. (5)

   (f) What do you think are the main pressures which celebrities face today? (10)

3. (a) Give an account of the conversation when Jesus asked his disciples questions about himself. (5)

   (b) Why did most of the people not recognise him as the Messiah? (5)

   (c) Imagine that you are a religious leader today. Write a new-year message for the nation in which you express your hopes for the coming year. (10)

4. (a) What did Peter offer to do at the time of the Transfiguration? (5)

   (b) Which two prophets appeared with Jesus on the mountain and what do you think they represented? (5)

   (c) The disciples were ordered not to tell anyone about this event and they obeyed. Your friend tells you something very exciting and asks you to keep it a secret. How easy would you find this? Is it always right to keep secrets? (10)

Scholarship Questions

1. Ten years ago a teacher asked a class of eleven year olds to write down the names of their heroes. Many wrote down the names of famous men and women who had spent their lives helping others or fighting against evil in their countries. Recently he repeated this exercise with children of the same age group. For the most part, the names written down were of sports stars, film or pop stars.

   (a) Why do you think that the two lists were so different? (7)

   (b) Do you think that the difference matters? Give reasons for your answer. (6)

   (c) Write a paragraph about someone you regard as a hero, including why, for you, his or her life is special. (7)

2. *Does a person gain anything if he wins the whole world yet loses his life?* (Mark 8 v 36)

   (a) On which occasion did Jesus say these words? (8)

   (b) What do you think he meant by them? (12)

3. The climax of *St Mark's Gospel* is Peter's profession of faith: *'You are the Messiah.'* (Mark 8 v 29)

   Explain fully why such a claim was beset by complications, and why Jesus chose to keep his identity a secret. (20)

6

PARABLES

THE GOOD SAMARITAN

LUKE 10 vv 25–37

His heart was filled with pity (Luke 10 v 33)

A NOTE ON PARABLES

A parable is a story with a meaning. Jesus told parables to teach people about God and to provoke them into thinking about God in new ways. Jesus' parables use events from the daily lives of the people he was speaking to. Notice just how few words he uses and yet how vivid the stories are.

SUMMARY OF THE TEXT

A teacher of the Law asked Jesus what he must do to receive eternal life.

Jesus replied that he must love God and his neighbour as much as he loved himself.

The lawyer asked, 'Who is my neighbour?'

It was in answer to this question that Jesus told the following parable:

A man journeying from Jerusalem to Jericho was violently robbed and left for dead.

In turn a priest and Levite saw him, but passed by on the other side of the road.

But a Samaritan, on seeing the victim, was moved with compassion to help him.

He tended his wounds, put him on his ass and took him to an inn.

After spending the night with the injured man, he left him in the care of the innkeeper, handing over money to cover any further expenses.

Jesus then asked the lawyer which man he considered to be a neighbour to the man who had been attacked.

The lawyer replied, 'The one who was kind to him.'

Jesus then told the lawyer to go and behave in the same way.

COMMENTARY ON THE TEXT

The Old Testament books of *Exodus, Leviticus, Deuteronomy* and *Numbers* contain 613 commandments (Torah) which cover everything in life from the big things, such as murder and stealing, to what you should eat and what you should do with mildew in the house! *(Leviticus 14 v 33)* The Jewish name for this collection of rules is the *Torah* which is translated as the *Law*.

In the Jewish community of Jesus' day the lawyer would be an expert on the detail of these commandments.

It is important not to think that following the Torah was totally misguided. Jews today still regard these laws as a wonderful gift from God, as a guide for living and a way to be near Him.

Psalm 119

> *Happy are those whose lives are faultless,*
> *who live according to the Law of the Lord*
> *Happy are they who obey his commands,*
> *who obey him with all their heart.*

Jesus would have certainly felt the same about the Law. It was not a burden but a source of joy. As the Psalm put it, the result of keeping the Law is happiness.

However, as we have seen, Jesus was more than ready to speak out and to act when he saw that the strict practice of these rules got in the way of doing good.

the lawyer's motive

The lawyer here was testing Jesus to see if he knew his Law well enough to be a proper teacher. When the lawyer mentioned eternal life in his question, he was not asking what he had to do to qualify for Heaven. His question meant that he was wondering what he should do in order to be always close to God, that is, which laws should he keep.

Jesus' reply

Jesus' first reply sent the lawyer to the Scriptures to find an answer to his own question. This was a good answer for Jesus to give and would not have upset anyone. The lawyer's summary of the Law was an excellent answer too. This summary is still used in Christian worship.

v 24 *Love God and love your neighbour as you love yourself.*

This is a combined quotation from the Old Testament books of *Deuteronomy 6 v 5* and *Leviticus 19 v 18*.

The lawyer's follow-up question was more testing. He asked Jesus, 'Who is my neighbour?' meaning, 'Who do I have a duty to care about?' For, as an expert in the Law, he would follow very strict guidelines about whom he would and would not speak to, eat with or touch.

In some ways this strict attitude is not surprising, when you think of how the Jewish people were surrounded by other cultures and actually oppressed by one. They would be very anxious to keep themselves to themselves, in order to protect their religion and culture.

The priest and the Levite

Herod's great Temple was begun around 20 BC and was still not complete when the Romans wrecked it in AD 70. It is often mentioned in the *Gospels* and its remains can still be seen in Jerusalem today.

The chief purpose of the Temple was to be a holy place where priests could carry out the sacrifices to God which were required at certain times of the year and at certain moments in life. The job of a priest was passed on from father to son. Families with certain names were automatically priestly families. The family Levi was one such family. So the Levite who also passed by was a priest also. The priest and the Levite were both important officials from the Temple in Jerusalem.

vv 31–32 . . . they walked on by, on the other side.

The most probable reason for this is that if the victim were indeed dead, then they would have become 'unclean' by touching him. Touching a dead body, according to Jewish custom, made a person unclean. Such uncleanliness would require days of special washing and prayers. This most certainly would have hindered their work in the Temple.

Those listening to this parable for the first time would be shocked by its content. They would not expect to hear in a story that Temple officials failed in their duty. The crowd would be thinking: 'Where is this leading? – No priest or Levite would walk past an injured man!' Worse was to follow. Little would they dream that the hero of the story would be a Samaritan!

Samaritans

Samaria was a neighbouring country *(see map on page 106)*. Its people followed the Jewish faith but were regarded as outcasts by the Jewish people. This is because many of them had married partners from other cultures, so, in the eyes of those listening to Jesus, Samaritans were outcasts with whom no social contact was permitted.

v 33 . . . and when he saw him, his heart was filled with pity.

That a Samaritan would go to the injured man would have really made Jesus' listeners angry, especially on top of the first insult to their religious leaders. Jesus wanted to shock them into the truth that feelings of compassion and willingness to care for others must not depend upon their colour, their race, religion or anything else.

The Good Samaritan not only gave first aid, he put the man on his donkey, took him to an inn and spent the night nursing him. He then left money for further help if necessary. Remember he did all this for someone he did not even know – an unconscious foreigner who most likely would have hated him on sight!

v 36 Which one of these three acted like a neighbour . . .?

The lawyer could not even bring himself to say the word *Samaritan*. He simply replied: 'The one who was kind to him.'

The lawyer's original question could be restated by anyone who wanted to be a follower of Jesus as: 'To whom can I be a neighbour?'

Jesus' answer was: 'You must be a neighbour to anyone who is in need, not just your family, friends or those of the same religion, those with the same coloured skin or with the same taste in music and clothes. Everyone is your neighbour!'

Questions on the Commentary

1. Explain what is meant by the word *parable*.

2. What was the work of

   (i)   the lawyer

   (ii) the priest and the Levite?

3. (i)   Why did the lawyer question Jesus in the first place?

   (ii) What good answer did the lawyer first offer to Jesus' question?

4. Give **two** reasons why those who listened to this parable for the first time would not have enjoyed it.

5. What is the message of this parable?

CONTEMPORARY ISSUES

A MODERN GOOD SAMARITAN

The phrase *Good Samaritan* has passed into everyday usage to describe someone who does a good turn. The newspapers used it for this story:

> *In the 1970s, teenage boys who followed punk rock bands looked fearsome. They had spiky, brightly-coloured hair and wore black leather from head to toe. They also had pierced ears with chains leading to pierced noses. At this time a London underground train crashed and a woman was trapped under the seats of a dark,*

wrecked carriage. When the firemen came to rescue her, they found that she had been comforted and had had her hand held all this time by a punk rocker who could have crawled to safety and freedom from the wreckage.

1. Why do you think this part of the crash story was published in the newspapers?

2. Write a newspaper article with the details of this story under a headline which links it with the Bible story.

3. Design a poster with the title LOVE YOUR NEIGHBOUR.

4. In groups of six, re-enact this parable.

5. Rewrite this parable in modern-day terms. Replace the priest and Levite with people in modern professions and the Samaritan by someone who is an outcast from our society.

Common Entrance Questions

1. (a) What is a parable? (1)

   (b) In one of his parables Jesus tells of a man who was attacked and beaten up on the road from Jerusalem to Jericho. Who passed by the injured man, not offering to help? (2)

   (c) He told this parable to answer a question from a teacher of the Law. What was that question? (2)

   (d) Describe what the Samaritan did to help the man. (5)

   (e) Explain the meaning of this parable. (5)

   (f) Retell this parable for today's world. (10)

2. *It so happened that a priest was going down that road; but when he saw the man, he walked on by, on the other side.* (Luke 10 v 31)

   (a) Why do you think he passed by? (5)

   (b) Describe what happened next in the story. (10)

   (c) Provide a detailed example from your own or someone else's experience when you or they passed by on the other side. Try to explain why this happened. (10)

3. *The next day he took out two silver coins and gave them to the innkeeper.* (Luke 10 v 35)

   (a) Explain why those hearing this story for the first time might have been upset. (5)

   (b) What was Jesus' message in the parable? (5)

   (c) Give full details of any charitable work with which you, your family or your school is involved. Explain not the method of fund-raising used, but rather what the money raised is used for. (10)

Scholarship Questions

1. Are all prejudices wrong?   (20)

2. A teacher of the law asked Jesus, 'Who is my neighbour?'

    (a) What answer was he expecting?   (5)

    (b) Why did he not like the answer which Jesus gave?   (5)

    (c) What would you say in answer to the lawyer's question?   (10)

3. Provide the biographical details of a life which you would say would qualify
    for the title *A Twentieth Century Good Samaritan.*   (20)

THE LOST SON

LUKE 15 vv 11–32

But now he is alive (Luke 15 v 32)

SUMMARY OF THE TEXT

A father had two sons.

One day the younger son asked him for his share of the money that would normally come to him after his father's death.

The father gave it to him and he immediately went off and before long spent it all.

He became so poor that he was forced to live with pigs and eat their food.

At last he came to his senses and decided to go home and apologise to his father.

He set off for home.

But when he was still far off, his father ran to meet him.

After hugging and kissing his son, who did not get a chance even to say sorry, the father decided to throw a huge party to celebrate his younger son's return.

The noise of the party led the older brother to find out what was going on.

He furiously accused his father of being totally unfair and completely wrong in rewarding his rogue of a brother in such an extravagant way.

His father calmly reminded his elder son that, now, all that he had belonged to his brother, and he invited him to come and join in the celebrations for the return of the lost son.

COMMENTARY ON THE TEXT

This parable used to be known as that of *The Prodigal Son*. The word *prodigal* means to be a recklessly wasteful spendthrift. This old title of the parable still turns up, either as a spoken saying or in stories which describe a wayward family member.

There is a real sense in which the story could be renamed *The Lost Sons* because, given the anger and resentment of the older son, it looks as though by the end of the story the father has lost him too! The older son appears to have no feeling whatsoever for his father's obvious lasting grief at the loss of his younger brother or for his joy at the prodigal's return!

v 12 . . . *give me my share of the property now.*

At this time, according to Jewish custom, a son did have the right to make this request. However, such an action would have cut him off from being part of the family. Hence the father's words at the end of the story: *My son was dead, and now he is alive.*

v 15 . . . *who sent him out to his farm to take care of the pigs.*

These words reveal the depths to which the boy had sunk. For the Jew, the pig was an unclean animal which must not be eaten or touched. Clearly, by working with pigs, he had put himself outside the Jewish community, as well as his family.

Amongst the pigs, the boy practised his apology which he would not need to say out loud because:

v 20 He was still a long way from home when his father saw him; his heart was filled

178

with pity, and he ran, threw his arms round his son, and kissed him.

These actions show that the father, despite the hurt and pain caused by the son's leaving home, had not stopped loving him. The father ran, not caring about the loss of dignity produced by his need to hitch up his long robe to be able to run. The boy was smothered in hugs before he could say the words he had rehearsed in front of the pigs.

v 28 The elder brother was so angry, he would not go into the house.

The elder son's views would be those of some of the bystanders. The younger brother was an irresponsible wastrel who deserved to be taught a lesson, not to have the prize calf killed in his honour!

The meaning of the parable

The father in the parable represents God. Just as the father readily forgave his son, because he loved him, so too, with God, when we are sorry, He will just as eagerly forgive us.

If an earthly father's love can so readily forgive, how much more will a heavenly father's love forgive. Furthermore, Jesus wanted the people of his time to welcome back into their community those whom they had made outcasts.

Questions on the Commentary

1. By which name was this parable formerly known?

2. Divide into groups of four and re-enact the story.

3. How does the parable show

    (i) the depths to which the lost son sank

    (ii) the readiness of the father's forgiveness?

CONTEMPORARY ISSUES

FORGIVENESS

(i) Nelson Mandela, the first black president of South Africa

Nelson Mandela spent twenty-seven years in prison. His crime was to argue for equal rights for black people in South Africa. At that time, all those in the white government believed in the evil system of apartheid. This separated the blacks from the whites in every aspect of life. They even had park benches and ambulances for whites only! Nelson Mandela was released from prison in 1990. At the moment of release he described his feelings towards his jailer, warrant officer James Gregory:

> As I left, I embraced him warmly. In the years he had looked after me . . . we had never discussed politics . . . but our bond was an unspoken one and I would miss his soothing presence. Men like him reinforced my belief in the humanity even of those who had kept me behind bars for the previous twenty-seven and a half years.

When Nelson was made President of South Africa, his jailer, warrant officer Gregory, was invited to the ceremony.

1. Why was Nelson Mandela put in prison for so long?

2. What is meant by *apartheid?*

3. What did Nelson see in his guards which enabled him to forgive them?

4. What final gesture of forgiveness did Nelson make to his guard?

(ii) John Wilson

While in Singapore in 1943 John Wilson was captured by the Japanese and accused of spying. He was tortured by them very severely. As the torture was going on, he thought of Jesus' crucifixion and how Jesus spoke words of forgiveness to those who crucified him. In his diary afterwards he wrote:

> I could not bring myself to use Jesus' words but I felt them. I said, 'Father, I know these men are doing their duty. Help them to see I am innocent'. I looked at their

faces as they stood around and took turns to flog me. They were hard and cruel and some were clearly enjoying what they were doing. But I managed to begin to see them as they once were – little children playing with their brothers and sisters and happy in their parents' love . . . it's hard to hate children.

1. As John was being tortured, what was his first prayer?

2. Why do you think he could not bring himself to use Jesus' actual words of forgiveness?

3. What final thought helped him through the ordeal of his torture?

(iii) **A lesson I'll never forget**

A teacher wrote the following about his most memorable lesson:

It was an East End of London school: twenty-five thirteen-year-old boys, half of them as big as me. RS, period ten, on a Friday. Everyone was always shattered – me included. About once a month, to help us all through it, we would have circle time. We would discuss Life, Death, The Universe and Each Other. With twenty minutes to go, big John Gaymer suddenly began to sob and he pointed his finger angrily at Tony Ackerman.

'Yesterday was the worst day of my life, Ackerman. It's all your fault Ackerman . . . all your fault. You always say it to me, always say it: "Gay John" this and "Gay John" that. Yesterday was my birthday and it didn't stop. I am so fed up with being called gay all the time by you when I'm not!'

We were all amazed, open-mouthed, dumbstruck – but nothing could have prepared us for what happened next. The depth of John's feeling, his utter despair, somehow touched a spot in Ackerman that had probably not been reached before. We all looked on as more drama began to unfold before our ever-widening eyes. Ackerman began to cry too. Big, loud-mouthed Ackerman, the biggest of the lot. A-name-for-everyone Ackerman. Hide-if-you-see-him-coming Ackerman. Tears were running down Ackerman's face. 'I'm sorry, I'm sorry, I am really sorry. I had no idea it upset you: I just meant it as a joke, I'm really sorry . . .'

And then it happened – gradually each member of the group started to say what they didn't like and what names hurt them. 'Just because my ears are big, it doesn't mean to say I like being called Dumbo.' It suddenly wasn't last period

181

on a Friday: it was something else entirely.

1. Why do you think Ackerman apologised?

2. Write a few lines about what sort of boy you think Ackerman was.

3. Why do you think they all suddenly started to share their true feelings about each other?

4. What does the teacher mean by the words: *it was something else entirely*?

Common Entrance Questions

1. (a)   In the parable of the Lost Son, which son left home early with his inheritance? (1)

    (b)   What did this son do with his money? (2)

    (c)   What happened to this son in 'another country'? (2)

    (d)   Describe the reunion of the father and his lost son. (5)

    (e)   Explain the meaning of this parable. (5)

    (f)   'In this parable the real lessons are to be learnt from the behaviour of the elder son.' Do you agree with this statement? (10)

2. (a)   Retell *The Parable of the Lost Son* from the point of view of

    (i)   the older brother

    (ii)   the father. (15)

    (b)   Do you think it is harder to forgive members of your family or close friends? Give examples in your answer. (10)

3. (a)   Who asked the question: 'Who is my neighbour?' (1)

    (b)   In the *Parable of the Good Samaritan*, who passed the man who had been beaten up on the road from Jerusalem to Jericho? (1)

    (c)   What did the Samaritan do to help the injured man? (3)

    (d)   In the *Parable of the Lost Son*, why do you think the elder brother was annoyed? Give reasons. (5)

    (e)   Explain what you think these two parables tell us about Jesus. (5)

    (f)   There are many charities asking for our support. Which do you think are the most deserving? Give full reasons. (10)

Scholarship Questions

1. Discuss the suggestion made by an expert on the New Testament that *The Parable of the Lost Son* could also be called *The Parable of the Lost Sons*. (20)

2. 'It is easier to forgive friends than family.'

   (a) Retell the parable which comes to mind when you think about this statement. (8)

   (b) From you own experience, write in full your views about this. (12)

THE SOWER

LUKE 8 vv 4–8, 11–15

SUMMARY OF THE TEXT

Jesus told the following parable to a large crowd.

A sower scattered seed.

Four things happened to the seed.

Some fell on the path where it was trodden on and birds ate it.

Some fell onto rocks, where after sprouting, the plant died through lack of moisture.

Some fell among thorns where the young plants were choked by the thorns.

Finally some seed fell on good soil where it grew to bear corn, a hundred grains each.

Jesus then explained the meaning of the parable.

The seed is the word of God.

That which falls on the path to be eaten by birds represents the times when the Devil comes to take God's word from people's hearts.

The seed on the rocky ground stands for shallow people who hear and receive the word gladly at first but, at the first test of their faith, fall away.

The thorns stand for those whose life is crowded out by worries, riches and pleasures and God's word does not have a chance of bearing fruit.

The good soil stands for those who hear and retain the word of God with a good, obedient heart, so that it bears fruit richly in their lives.

COMMENTARY ON THE TEXT

It is clear that, for the Gospel writer, the sower represents Christ himself.

As ever with his parables, Jesus is using a very familiar example from the everyday experience of his hearers. They would all be familiar with this broadcast method of sowing seeds.

v 6 . . . *rocky ground* . . .

Soil in Galilee is sometimes very thin, barely covering the underlying limestone rock.

The point of the parable is that Jesus' words are like seeds sown in the ground. If you have faith in Jesus and accept his word, then your life will bear fruit accordingly. That is his message.

Jesus' disciples would also realise how difficult their task would be to make converts. For every one person who believed, there would be three others who did not.

Questions on the Commentary

1. When the sower sowed his seed, which **four** things happened to the seed?

2. What does the seed stand for in the parable?

3. What is the meaning of the seed falling among thorns?

4. In the parable, who does the sower represent?

5. What message about their future work would Jesus' disciples take from this parable?

Common Entrance Questions

1. (a) In *The Parable of the Sower*, what is the seed meant to represent? (1)

   (b) What happened to the seeds which fell on the path? (2)

   (c) What did the seeds which fell on the rocky ground represent? (2)

   (d) Give a brief account of another parable which Jesus told. (5)

   (e) Explain why Jesus used parables in his teaching. (5)

   (f) Sometimes we take up something in a burst of enthusiasm, only to drop it a little while later. Use your own experiences to write a modern version of *The Parable of the Sower*. (10)

2. (a) Who does the sower represent in the parable Jesus told? (1)

   (b) What does the seed represent in this parable? (1)

   (c) Why did Jesus use parables? (3)

   (d) Describe what happened to the seed the sower scattered. (5)

   (e) Explain the meaning which Jesus gave to this parable. (5)

   (f) Why might it be difficult to follow Jesus' teaching today? (10)

Scholarship Questions

1. Use your knowledge of the parables which Jesus told to sum up his teaching to mankind. (20)

2. Which of the parables which Jesus told do you think is the most relevant to today's world? (20)

3. 'Human beings are just as ready to believe anything as they ever were.' Do you think this statement is true? Give full reasoning in your answer. (20)

7

JESUS' TEACHING

THE SERMON ON THE PLAIN

LUKE 6 vv 17–49, LUKE 12 vv 22–31

SUMMARY OF THE TEXT

In the parable of *The Good Samaritan*, Jesus offered his followers a practical example of what he wanted them to do.

These verses provide the theory.

They cover:

- where true happiness lies

- love for enemies

- judging others

- the difference between good and bad people

- the parable of the two housebuilders

- trust in God

But just as the parable of *The Good Samaritan* shocked people with its contents, so does this teaching.

As rules for living, they seem to defy common sense.

COMMENTARY ON THE TEXT

Luke 6 v 20–26 *The Beatitudes*

This section is called the *Beatitudes* because in the early English version of the Bible each line of this section begins not with the words *Happy are* . . . but *Blessed are* and *beatus* is the Latin word for *blessed*.

v 20 *Happy are you poor: the Kingdom of God is yours!*

The message of the *Beatitudes* is one which Jesus often gave. Mankind cannot find deep happiness through things: possessions, designer clothes, Mercedes and Nintendos or even food and drink (remember, *man cannot live by bread alone . . .*). Jesus taught that lasting, deep happiness can only be found by finding God and living in relationship to Him.

v 22 *Happy are you when people hate you, reject you, insult you and say that you are evil, all because of the Son of Man.*

Not long after Jesus' death, his followers were persecuted (punished for their belief in him), firstly by the Jewish authorities and then for many years by the Romans.

The Romans considered their Emperors to be gods. To honour this decision, everyone had to drink a toast to the god Augustus. Those who did not were sent to the lions.

For the Christians who refused to toast the Emperor god, these verses provided comfort for them as they awaited their fate.

Son of Man

This is the title which Jesus most often used of himself. He was quoting from the Old Testament book of *Daniel chapter 7 v 13* where the prophet Daniel describes his vision of a figure in the clouds. Older versions of the Bible name this figure as Son of Man. In the *Good News Bible Daniel 7 vv 13–14* reads:

> *I saw what looked like a human being . . . he went to the one who had been living for ever and was presented to him. He was given authority, honour, and royal power, so that the people of all nations, races and languages would serve him. His authority would last for ever, and his kingdom would never end.*

This is the role which Jesus claimed for himself when he called himself *Son of Man.*

Luke 6 vv 27–38 *The Law of Love*

v 27 *. . . love your enemies, do good to those who hate you . . .*

This is Jesus' most important teaching. It is also his most difficult. Nations have never managed it and neither have most individuals. It is important, though, to understand what Jesus meant when he used the word *love*.

The *Gospels* were written in Greek. The Greek language is fortunate in that it has three words for three different meanings of our one word *love*. The Greek words are:

> **philos** which means love of friends

> **eros** which means sexual love between partners

> **agape** (pronounced *agapay*) means caring for others, no matter whether you know them or even like them. It is caring without any thought of the cost to self. This is the word for love which Jesus used when he said 'Love your neighbour.' It is the love which the Samaritan showed to a complete stranger. The victim was unconscious, so there is no question of the Samaritan having to like or to know the victim before he started to help him with his *agape*!

It is important then to understand just what sort of love Jesus meant because our single word for *love* has to cope with not only the three Greek meanings mentioned above, but everything ranging from loving chocolate pudding to the deepest love one can feel for another person!

An impossible teaching?

To love our enemies defies common sense! If someone hits you, your every instinct is to hit him back even if he is bigger than you are. But Jesus would say that returning violence with violence is simply adding to the evil in the world. It gives evil another victory.

As far as those listening to Jesus were concerned, they had enemy soldiers in their midst and they would find the teaching about turning the other cheek particularly hard to follow.

V 31 Do for others just what you want them to do for you.

This is known as *The Golden Rule*. It occurs in other religions too. For example, ancient Jewish teaching states:

> *What is hateful to you, do not do to your fellow.*

Does this way of writing the Golden Rule change its meaning in any way?

v 35 . . . you will be children of the Most High God.

Jesus was making a promise to those who followed his way of loving (*agape*) others. They would be as sons of God because the way of *agape* is the way of God. Elsewhere in the New Testament it says God is love (*agape*).

191

v 37 *Do not judge others . . . do not condemn others . . . forgive others . . .*

Then God will not judge or condemn you. And God will forgive you.

Jesus' teaching is different from that of the Eastern religions in which all your evil acts combine to produce bad *Karma* for you. Jesus taught that you can have a whole wealth of evil deeds behind you, yet the moment you turn to God for forgiveness, He runs, arms open wide, to hug you with extravagant forgiveness. Also, Jesus taught that we do not earn God's forgiveness by our good deeds. God's forgiveness is a natural result of His love for us, in the same way that the father could not help forgiving his lost son because he loved him.

Further, Jesus teaches that, if our heavenly father can forgive us with that sort of generosity, and does not condemn us, so we, for our part, should not condemn others but be equally generous in our forgiveness.

Luke 6 vv 46–49 *The need to set an example . . .*

Jesus expects those who follow him not to be hypocrites and, better still, to be known for their goodness and for their *agape.*

Luke 6 vv 46–49 *The Parable of the Two Houses*

v 46 *Why do you call me 'Lord, Lord' . . .?*

These words say much about the beliefs of those who followed Jesus. It shows that not only did they respect him as a teacher, but they had also come to realise that he was the Messiah.

v 47 *Anyone who comes to me and listens to my words and obeys them . . .*

Like the Old Testament prophets before him *(see the chapter on Amos),* Jesus was always ready to expose false religion. In this case it was a religion built upon words and not good deeds. A modern writer expressed this teaching of Jesus in the following words:

> *Your religion, quite simply, whether it is fancy or plain, is what you are when the talking stops and the action starts.*

Luke 12 vv 22–31

v 22 *. . . I tell you not to worry about the food you need . . . or about the clothes . . .*

Jesus teaches again that the most important concerns for humans should not be our food or our clothes, but the needs of the spirit. In the Kingdom which Jesus described, man is only fulfilled when he stops caring about his own self and begins wholeheartedly caring for others.

Questions on the Commentary

1. Why are the *Beatitudes* so called?

2. Who, in particular, would obtain great comfort from these verses?

3. What is meant by *persecution*? Give an example of it.

4. What is the main message of the *Beatitudes*?

5. Do you think the Greeks have an advantage in having three words for love?

6. What did Jesus mean by the word *love*?

7. Using materials / media of your own choice, design a poster for the wall which includes the words:

   DO TO OTHERS AS YOU WOULD WANT THEM TO DO TO YOU

CONTEMPORARY ISSUES

LOVE YOUR ENEMIES

(i) On 7 May 1915 Randall Davidson, the then Archbishop of Canterbury, wrote a letter of protest to the Prime Minister. The German army had started to use poisonous gas as a weapon. The Archbishop had heard that British troops were about to do the same. He wrote:

> *If anyone a few months ago had suggested that the British army would use poisonous gas to kill the enemy, no one would have believed them. What has happened to change our view? Nothing so far as I know, except that our enemy*

has sunk so low as to use it. They have degraded the traditions of military honour. Are we to do the same? If they go on to poison the wells of villagers, will we follow suit? If so, can we retain self-respect on the part of the army or the Nation?

His letter was ignored and a horrendous war continued with a terrible loss of life on both sides. Nations have never been able to love their enemies, although individuals have.

1. Why did Randall Davidson write to the Prime Minister?

2. Imagine you are the Prime Minister. Write a reply to Randall Davidson.

(ii)   A Russian poet wrote about the time near the end of World War Two:

The people of a war-torn Russian village lined the pavements to jeer and spit at their enemy: the German prisoners of war who were to be paraded down the main street.

When eventually they came, the jeering gradually subsided, as it was more than obvious by their ragged clothes and skeletal bodies, that the enemy looked more starved even than they were. Suddenly an old woman stepped forward and thrust a crust of bread into the hands of a very young, half-dead-looking German boy soldier who was being held up by his comrades. From the now silent crowd, slowly but surely other hands began to appear with tiny offerings for fellow sufferers . . .

1.   What changed the villagers' attitudes to the Germans?

2.   Write a diary entry for the day for

      either   (a)   the old Russian lady who gave the crust

      or   (b)   the young German soldier who received it.

Common Entrance Questions

1. (a) In Jesus' *Beatitudes*, what reward will the poor receive? (1)

   (b) Name **two** other types of people who receive rewards in these verses. (2)

   (c) According to the teaching of Jesus, what should you do if someone hits you on the right cheek? (2)

   (d) What does Jesus teach about not judging others? (5)

   (e) Explain the meaning of Jesus' parable about two house builders. (5)

   (f) 'Jesus' teaching is too difficult for most to carry out.' Do you agree? Give reasons for your answer. (10)

2. (a) Retell, in your own words, the parable of the two men who built houses. (10)

   (b) What was the point of this parable of Jesus? (5)

   (c) What value has this message for today's world? (10)

3. (a) Which rewards did Jesus say the poor would have? (1)

   (b) What did Jesus say we should do to our enemies? (1)

   (c) What was the message behind Jesus' short parable about two house builders? (3)

   (d) Summarise, in your own words, Jesus' teaching on trusting in God. (5)

   (e) Explain why many people throughout history have found the teaching of Jesus very difficult to follow. Give your reasons. (5)

   (f) Do you think there is ever a right reason to go to war? Give examples. (10)

Scholarship Questions

1. *Happy are you poor: the Kingdom of God is yours.*

   What do you think Jesus meant by the *Kingdom of God*? (20)

2. (a) Explain fully what Jesus meant by his parable about two men who each built a house differently. (8)

   (b) Does this teaching have any value in the third millennium AD? (12)

3. *Love your enemies, do good to them that hate you.*

   Do these words of Jesus mean that all Christians should be pacifists? (20)

4. If the evil rulers of the twentieth century, such as Stalin and Hitler, had repented on their deathbeds, should God have forgiven them? (20)

8

THE SENTENCE, CRUCIFIXION AND BURIAL

MARK 15 vv 6–47

SUMMARY OF THE TEXT

The text included for study begins after Jesus has appeared in a trial chaired by the High Priest.

Jesus was then passed on to the Roman governor Pontius Pilate who reminded the crowd of the Passover tradition whereby he could free a prisoner of their choice.

Believing that the religious leaders had arrested Jesus out of jealousy, Pilate allowed the crowd to choose between Barabbas, a murderer, or Jesus.

The crowd had been stirred up to shout for Barabbas' release and, when Pilate asked the crowd what should be done with Jesus, they shouted, 'Crucify him.'

Pilate, wishing to keep the crowd happy, had Jesus flogged and handed him over to be crucified.

The soldiers who dressed him as a king then mocked Jesus.

They put a purple robe and crown of thorns on him.

They spat on him, beat him and pretended to bow, saying, 'Hail, King of the Jews.'

When Jesus was on the way to be crucified, the soldiers forced Simon of Cyrene to carry Jesus' cross.

When they arrived at Golgatha, the place of execution, Jesus refused wine drugged with myrrh.

The soldiers then shared Jesus' clothes between them, using a die to see who won which items of his clothes.

At nine o'clock they crucified him.

They nailed a notice to his cross which read 'King of the Jews'.

Two bandits were crucified either side of him and with others they mocked Jesus.

At noon there was darkness.

At three o'clock Jesus cried out and some of the bystanders thought that he had called Elijah.

When Jesus died, the curtain in the Temple became torn in two, and a Roman soldier, who had witnessed the crucifixion, at that moment believed that Jesus was the Son of God.

As it was the day before the Sabbath, Joseph of Arimathea went to Pilate to ask for Jesus' body.

Pilate was surprised that Jesus had died so soon and, having verified that Jesus had died, he granted Joseph's request.

Jesus was taken down from the cross and laid in a tomb cut out of the rock.

A stone was rolled across its entrance.

COMMENTARY ON THE TEXT

The charge against Jesus was that he claimed to be the King of the Jews and it is as such that he was handed over for execution.

There is some discussion among scholars as to whether the Jewish authorities had the power of the death penalty.

The fact that Jesus had to appear before Pilate might be evidence that they could not execute Jesus themselves. The Jewish religious leaders knew full well that the Romans would be only too keen to execute someone who claimed to be a king and therefore a rival to the rule of Caesar.

v 14 'But what crime has he committed?' Pilate asked.

Mark has clearly shown that Jesus' trial before the High Priest was a mockery of justice. He also presents Pilate as being aware that the charges against Jesus were false.

However, the idea that Pilate was somehow a weak and easily-swayed leader does not fit in with what is known from Roman history about Pontius Pilate.

The Jews were a troublesome people to rule and the Emperor had to make sure that there was someone tough enough for the job. From all accounts, Pilate was such a man and was a ruthless, feared and hated Procurator. Pontius Pilate would not think twice, therefore, about sending someone like Jesus to his death.

This fact is actually recorded in Roman history as well as the Gospels. The historian *Tacitus* wrote in a very hostile way about Christianity which he calls *a deadly superstition*:

> *Christus . . . suffered the extreme penalty during the reign of Tiberius at the hands of one of our procurators, Pontius Pilatus, and a deadly superstition broke out not only in Judaea, the first source of the evil, but also in the City (Rome) where all things shameful from every part of the world meet and become popular.*

Mark presented Pilate as knowing Jesus to be innocent. Mark's motive in doing this was probably that he wanted to lay the blame of Jesus' death firmly at the door of the Jewish religious leaders who had so dramatically rejected God's Messiah.

v 15 Then he had Jesus whipped . . .

Flogging was normal before crucifixion. It was very savage. The whip was leather and attached to its thongs were pieces of metal and bone.

v 17 They dressed him in purple.

This is the colour which was worn by emperors. The crown of thorns was an imitation of the crown of the sun god from which the sun's rays flowed. Pictures of such god-like rulers were on the coins of the time.

The soldiers' mockery and the notice 'King of the Jews' which they would nail to the cross is of course ironical. For Mark and all Christians, Jesus *was* King of the Jews.

Crucifixion was a very cruel and slow execution, widely practised in the ancient world. It was used by the Romans for slaves and the worst kind of criminal. They also used it for those who rebelled against Roman rule. The victim was stripped naked and fixed by nails to suffer torments of pain, thirst, insects and taunts.

Death came slowly as a result of exhaustion when the victim did not have any strength left to lift up his chest to breathe. In all it was an agonising, humiliating and a very slow way to die.

v 21 *. . . and the soldiers forced . . . (Simon of Cyrene) to carry Jesus' cross.*

Criminals usually had to carry their own cross beam which would be then fixed to the upright post at the place of crucifixion. Mark does not explain why Simon was made to carry Jesus' cross beam. More than likely it was because Jesus was by then too weak to carry his own.

v 22 *Golgatha*

The language which Jesus would have spoken is Aramaic. The word *Golgatha* in Aramaic means *skull*. This suggests that the place of crucifixion was a skull-shaped hill or simply that it was a place of death.

v 23 *They tried to give him wine mixed with a drug called myrrh . . .*

This would have been offered to Jesus probably by the women who were his followers rather than by the Roman soldiers. It would have the effect of reducing the pain. In a similar way, before anaesthetics were invented, sometimes patients would be offered alcohol before surgery. The fact that Jesus refused this is a sign that he accepted this path of suffering as God's will for him.

v 24 *Then they crucified him and divided his clothes among themselves . . .*

Jesus' arms and feet would have been fixed to the cross with rope and nails. The clothes of the victim became the property of the executioners, one of the 'perks' of the job. They would throw dice for the best pieces.

v 26 *The notice of the accusation against him said 'King of the Jews'.*

Crucifixions normally happened in a public place with an inscription pinned to the cross so that passers-by would know why the criminal was being executed. The Romans naturally hoped this slow, horrible death for the publicised crime would deter others from doing the same.

Jesus' notice was of course put there by the authorities in sarcasm, but for Mark the sign above the cross revealed a deep truth. For the Gospel writer, the proof of Jesus' kingship lay in his path of suffering even as far as the cross.

The idea of the cross as a sort of throne is sometimes seen in churches where Jesus is shown on the cross in kingly robes wearing a crown. This is very different from the more usual cross upon which is placed an almost naked human figure, or no figure at all – an empty cross. Each of the three crosses symbolises a different aspect of the Easter story.

v 27 *They also crucified two bandits with Jesus, one on his right, the other on his left.*

The request to have the places of honour (to be at Jesus' right and left) was fulfilled by two criminals. This was the moment which Jesus pointed to when his two disciples asked to have the best places in his kingdom.

v 29 *People passing by shook their heads and hurled insults at Jesus.*

Mark shows three groups of people mocking Jesus: the passers-by (shaking their heads was a gesture of contempt), the religious leaders (chief priests, scribes) and the criminals on either side of him.

So, surrounded by jeering, Mark provides us with a scene where Jesus is completely alone on the cross. This is heightened by Jesus' cry:

v 34 *Eloi, Eloi lema sabachthani,* which means, *My God, my God, why did you abandon me?*

These words are a direct quotation from the opening of *Psalm 22*. It is not surprising that, in such an extreme of physical and mental agony, Jesus would use the Bible for comfort. This psalm begins with these words of despair but it ends with words of faith and hope about God. Christians always see these words of Jesus as proof that he was truly a human being as well as God's Messiah.

v 35 . . . *'Listen, he is calling for Elijah.'*

The great Old Testament prophet, Elijah, was seen as a bringer of comfort to good people who were suffering. He was also the person who the Jews thought would herald the arrival of the Messiah.

v 38 *The curtain hanging in the Temple was torn in two from top to bottom.*

The most sacred place in the Temple, the Holy of Holies, was covered by a curtain. Only once a year the High Priest was allowed to pass through it. Its tearing at the moment of Jesus' death has possibly two meanings:

- It is a sign of the judgement to come on the Jewish religious leaders who rejected Jesus. The Temple was destroyed by Rome in AD 70.

- It symbolises the opening up of God's Kingdom. Jesus came not just to call the people of Israel but all mankind. The Roman soldier's faith at the moment of Jesus' death makes the same point: God's Kingdom is open to Gentiles as well as to Jews.

v 40 *Some women . . .*

It was not Jesus' Apostles who were at the foot of the cross but women. *(See the notes on Mary Magdalene in the next chapter.)* However, in John's version of the crucifixion, John himself was present at the foot of the cross *(John 19 vv 25–27).*

The story of Jesus' burial was important since it confirmed that he really did die on the cross.

v 43 *It was Preparation day (that is the day before the Sabbath) . . .*

When possible, burials had to take place on the day of death and on the following day at the latest, so that a death late on Friday evening required instant action. Jewish law also insisted that a criminal's corpse had to be buried before nightfall, in case it brought a curse to the land.

v 46 *. . . and placed it in a tomb which had been dug out of solid rock.*

Rock-hewn tombs were common in the area and the use of a stone to seal the entrance to a tomb was normal. The mention of the women present at the burial serves to place them as witnesses to where Jesus' body had been taken.

Questions on the Commentary

1. For which types of criminal did the Romans use crucifixion as a method of execution?

2. How did crucifixion bring about the death of the victim?

3. Copy out this sentence with the missing words correctly placed in it:

   Simon of .... carried Jesus' cross because ....

   ....

4. Why did the Romans put inscriptions above their crosses?

5. Which groups of people mocked Jesus when he was on the cross?

6. Find photographs or paintings of each of the **three** different kinds of cross which may be found inside a church. Which different aspect of the Easter message does each cross symbolise?

7. Read *Psalm 22*. What are the links in the first part of this psalm with what happened to Jesus?

8. When Jesus died on the cross, *Mark's Gospel* records that the curtain of the Temple was torn in two. What did this symbolise?

9. Why is Tacitus' description of Jesus' being condemned by Pilate good evidence that Jesus really existed?

CONTEMPORARY ISSUES

EXECUTION

(i) As the power of the Nazi party spread in Germany, some people recognised its evil aims. One such man was a colonel in the German Army, Alexis von Roenne. He was accused of being involved in the 1944 plot to overthrow Hitler and was condemned to death. The day before his execution he wrote a long letter to his mother. Below is an extract from it:

> *. . . For a week now I have been awaiting death from day to day; right now, for example, I expect it tomorrow, and the Saviour in his boundless mercy has freed me from all terror.*

> *I have a good appetite, I take pleasure in the sunshine and I sleep very peacefully and soundly like a child, the whole night through. One thing has helped me face tomorrow. When I think of how slowly Jesus had to die on the cross, my end will be much quicker than that or than some of the painful illnesses I might have had to endure, if I had lived.*

> *I have of course brought my little ones* (his two small children) *before God in my prayers. How good it is to think of such a large family who will love and care for you and them after I have gone.*

> *For this and for all the boundless love of nearly forty-two years, I thank you, my indescribably beloved mother, from the depth of my heart.*

1. What evidence does the letter give that Alexis was 'free from terror'?

2. What thoughts helped him face his own execution the next day?

3. What does the letter tell you about his family life?

4. Write about a difficult time when either you were helped by family and friends or when, by being a good friend, you supported someone else.

(ii) Albert Pierrepoint was Britain's last executioner. He was so good at his job that he was picked to execute the convicted Nazi war criminals after the Nuremburg trials which took place at the end of World War Two.

In his autobiography he wrote that he was such an expert at his job that it only took fifteen seconds from the moment he shook hands and said 'Good morning' to the condemned person to the moment when that person was pronounced dead by the prison doctor!

On the subject of whether hanging people for murder actually deterred others from doing the same, he had firm views. He wrote:

> *It is said to be a deterrent. I cannot agree . . . If death were a deterrent, I would be expected to know. It is I who have faced them last, young lads and girls, working men, grandmothers. I have been amazed to see the courage with which they take that walk into the unknown. It did not deter them then, and it had not deterred them when they committed what they were convicted for.*

1. What were Albert Pierrepoint's reasons for his firm views?

2. Give your view in full as to whether it is ever right to execute another human being.

Common Entrance Questions

1. (a) Which Jewish festival was being celebrated at the time of Jesus' death? (1)

   (b) Who sentenced Jesus to death? Give his name and position. (2)

   (c) Who was released instead of Jesus? Give his name and status. (2)

   (d) Describe what the soldiers did to Jesus before he was crucified. (5)

   (e) Explain the part played by Joseph of Arimathea in the burial of Jesus. (5)

   (f) Do you think that there is any crime today which deserves the death penalty? Give full reasons for your opinion. (10)

2. (a) Who dressed Jesus in a purple robe and a crown of thorns? (1)

   (b) Who carried Jesus' cross for him, and why? (2)

   (c) What was written on the notice which was nailed to Jesus' cross? (2)

   (d) Describe briefly the events which happened after Jesus was nailed to the cross, up to and including his death. (5)

   (e) In *Mark's Gospel* the army officer who saw Jesus die said, 'This man was really the Son of God.' Explain what you think led him to this conclusion. Give your reasons. (5)

   (f) To what extent do you agree or disagree with the use of the death penalty as a punishment today? (10)

2. (a) Tell the story of the crucifixion from the point of view of

   either   (i)   a Roman soldier

   or   (ii)   one of the chief priests. (15)

   (b) The soldiers involved in the herding of Jewish families into the death camps in World War Two said afterwards that they were simply obeying orders. Is that a good enough excuse for what they did? (10)

Scholarship Questions

1. (a) Why was Jesus crucified?   (10)

   (b) Is there anything worth giving your life for?   (10)

2. (a) In what sense was Jesus *King of the Jews*?   (8)

   (b) From what does the world today need saving?   (12)

3. Did Jesus need to die?   (20)

9

THE RESURRECTION

JOHN 20 vv 1–18

SUMMARY OF THE TEXT

Early on the Sunday morning, when Mary Magdalene went to the tomb, she found the stone moved and the tomb empty.

She immediately ran to tell the disciples.

The disciples then ran to the tomb as well and they too saw the empty tomb, noticing that the burial clothes had been carefully arranged.

Then the disciples went back home, leaving Mary alone outside the tomb.

She began a conversation with someone she supposed to be a gardener, but when he said her name, 'Mary', she immediately recognised him as Jesus.

Jesus then told Mary not to keep him there, but to go and tell the others the news of his resurrection.

COMMENTARY ON THE TEXT

Mary Magdalene

Mary had been a follower of Jesus since she had been cured of 'evil spirits'. This story is told in *Luke's Gospel*. In *Luke 8 v 2* we read:

Mary (who was called Magdalene) from whom seven demons had been driven out . . .

Another story in the same Gospel tells of a woman who had led a very sinful life. She caused a scandal by bringing Jesus expensive perfume in Simon the Pharisee's house. After this she washed Jesus' feet with her tears. However, this woman is not named in the story *(Luke 7 v 37)*. But the tradition that it was Mary Magdalene goes back a long time in Christian writing, probably because it fits what we know about Jesus' attitude to outcasts. He certainly would not have minded appearing first on Easter morning to a woman who had been a great sinner.

v 2 *They have taken the Lord from the tomb, and we don't know where they have put him!*

Mary's first thought on finding the tomb empty was that it had been broken open by tomb robbers – not an uncommon occurrence in those days.

She went running to Simon Peter and the other disciple, whom Jesus loved . . .

This 'other disciple whom Jesus loved' is mentioned several times in *John's Gospel.* Early Christian writing names him as John, son of Zebedee, brother of James. The same tradition believes this disciple to be the author of *John's Gospel.*

When Peter went into the tomb and found it empty, the text does not say what conclusion he reached. However, when the 'other disciple' went in, the text does provide which conclusion he came to when he saw the empty tomb.

v 8 *. . . he saw and believed.*

That is, he believed that Jesus had risen from the dead. This is the belief upon which the Christian faith is built.

The empty tomb in itself, of course, did not prove that Jesus had risen. His body could have been removed by his disciples or by grave robbers.

After the disciples had left, Mary remained alone at the tomb. When she looked inside it again, it was no longer empty. Two angels were there. She presumably did not recognise them as angels, because she said to them:

v 2 *They have taken my Lord away and I do not know where they have put him.*

v 16 *Jesus said to her, 'Mary!'*

Mary thought that Jesus was the gardener until he said her name. Only then did she recognise him. Earlier in this Gospel *(John 10 v 3)* Jesus calls himself the *Good Shepherd* who knows the names of those who love him. He calls them by their names, just as a good shepherd knows each of his sheep by name.

v 17 *Do not hold on to me . . .*

It is not very clear why Jesus said this. The reason he gave, 'I have not yet gone back up to the Father,' points to his final departure from his followers, an event which Christians call *The Ascension.*

It may be that the risen body of Jesus was in a form that could not be held.

It is difficult to get a consistent picture of what Jesus' risen body was like.

In *John 20 v 26* he writes that the disciples were behind closed doors, yet Jesus appeared among them. This points to a ghostly body which can materialise and dematerialise at will.

Yet in *John 20 v 27*, Thomas, who doubted that Jesus had risen, was able to touch the wounds of crucifixion in Jesus' risen body and in *John 21 v 13* Jesus actually appears on the shore to eat bread and fish with the disciples.

'Do not hold onto me' could also mean, 'do not hold onto my physical presence, let my body go because you and all my followers will be given the gift of my Spirit, something much better than my human form.'

The importance of the Resurrection

As we have seen, the empty tomb in itself did not prove that Jesus had risen from the dead. The proof for Christians is that during the days following that first Easter Sunday, Jesus made several appearances to his disciples.

This experience completely transformed his dejected followers. These men and women, who had seen their leader die a horrible, slow death, now became people who could not wait to preach the good news of their risen Lord.

Without the empty tomb, Christians say this could not have happened. For the four Gospel writers, of course, the fact that Jesus rose from the dead is the final proof that all they had written about him was true. Jesus truly was God's Messiah.

Questions on the Commentary

1. How did Mary come to be a follower of Jesus and with whom is her name linked?

2. What did Mary Magdalene first think when she saw that the tomb was empty?

3. Who was 'the other disciple whom Jesus loved'?

4. How in the end did Mary come to recognise Jesus?

5. How does this moment link to another part of *John's Gospel*?

6. Why is it difficult to have a clear idea about what Jesus' resurrected body was like?

7. Why is the empty tomb in itself not proof that Jesus rose from the dead?

CONTEMPORARY ISSUES

1. IS THERE SUCH A THING AS THE SUPERNATURAL?

(i) The Farmington Institute

Alistair Hardy decided to set up a research programme to find out how many people had had experiences which they could not explain. Such an experience might be a sense that something was going to happen just before it did, or a feeling of great calm and peace coming from nowhere, or the sight of a ghostly figure. He also believed that, for the most part, if the strange event only happened once, then the person would not tell anyone else. So he devised a questionnaire in which a question like this was asked:

> *Have you at any time in your life experienced something which you cannot explain, which you have not until now told anyone else about?*

The researchers were quite surprised to find that over sixty per cent of those interviewed answered 'Yes' to that question.

211

1. Give your views about this result, providing reasons why you are or are not surprised.

2. What do you think can be deduced from these findings?

3. Suggest how the research might be followed up or continued. Think of further questions.

4. Write your answer to the Hardy question.

(ii) Near-death experiences

There have been many occasions when patients either under an anaesthetic or when suffering from a grave illness at the point of death speak of their 'near-death experience'. After recovery, many report almost exactly the same things happening to them. They remember walking down a long tunnel towards a distant white light and some speak of meeting a figure who is welcoming to them. They usually speak of calm and peace and not of fear.

1. Why do you think that patients in this situation have similar experiences?

2. Do you think that these experiences are in any way proof of a life after death?

(iii) 'Are there ghosts, Piggy, or beasts?'

In William Golding's novel, *Lord of the Flies*, a group of boys aged between eight and thirteen are stranded on an island without adults. Things start well but soon, order breaks down as they begin to be afraid of a 'beast'. Ralph, the hero of the book, asks this question about ghosts to his wise friend Piggy who replies:

> *'Course there aren't.'*
> *'Why not?'*
> *''Cos things wouldn't make sense. Houses 'n streets, an' TV – they wouldn't work.'*

1. What do you think Piggy meant by his answer?

2. Do you believe in ghosts? Give full reasons for your opinion.

2. **FROM DEATH TO LIFE . . .**

Dave belonged to the Tuebrook Boot Boys, a street gang which met most evenings in a subway beneath West Derby Road, a busy dual carriageway between inner city Liverpool and its suburbs. Tuebrook was ugly with lots of boarded-up shops and graffiti on every bare patch of concrete.

Dave spent most of each morning in bed. After eating cold baked beans straight from the tin, he would make his way to the subway, looking for anyone else who was 'bunking off'. He couldn't remember the last time he had spent a whole week in school.

He was fourteen and looked twelve. Smoking as much as he did wouldn't help him grow, either, if his teacher was to be believed. For Dave, school was boring, home was boring and life only became remotely interesting when there was rumour of an attack from the Wavertree Clan, their hated rival gang. The meet for the fight was always Newsham Park but very little real fighting ever happened. It was mostly all bravado and rumour. Home, subway, park were Dave's world. In fact it was the same for all the 'bunkers' and all would have said, 'What's the point?' if anyone had suggested they go anywhere else.

Then it all changed. The Social Services decided that Dave, with other truants, should go for regular weekends to stay with youth workers in a hostel in North Wales. The shopkeepers in Betwys y Coed would lose pounds' worth of stock as Dave and his friends 'nicked' what they could before being chased out. But one weekend, when they were in Wales, Dave was made to go riding. He had only seen horses on TV before – but in reality they were quite something else . . .

The stable owner said Dave was a natural. His small body sat in the saddle as though he had been born there. Dave loved it. He loved horses. He loved the stable routine. Most of all he loved the riding. He begged to be able to stay and work there.

1. Make a list of the number of ways in which Dave's life in the city differs from yours.

2. Write an ending to this true story.

3. Design an Easter poster.

Common Entrance Questions

1. (a) When did Mary Magdalene visit the tomb of Jesus? (1)

    (b) What did she discover at the tomb? (2)

    (c) Who were the next people to visit the tomb? (2)

    (d) Describe what they found when they went inside the tomb. (5)

    (e) Jesus then appeared to Mary Magdalene. Briefly describe and explain her reaction. (5)

    (f) The story of Jesus' resurrection has been described as 'the greatest story ever told'. However, many people do not believe in it today. Explain why people reject this story and give your opinion (with reasons) of their arguments. (10)

2. (a) Who did Mary Magdalene see inside the tomb? (1)

    (b) At first, what did she think had happened? (2)

    (c) Why had Mary gone to the tomb in the first place? (2)

    (d) Describe the meeting between Mary and Jesus at the tomb. (5)

    (e) Explain the significance of Jesus' appearing to Mary Magdalene *before* he appeared to his disciples. (5)

    (f) 'The Resurrection of Jesus is still today the most important feature of the Christian religion.' Discuss this view. (10)

Scholarship Questions

1. What evidence do you think there is for life after death? (20)

2. What is the significance of the empty tomb for Christians? (20)

3. How important is the Easter story to the birth of Christianity? (20)

4. Can man make sense of his own life without the hope of eternal life? (20)

5. Do you think that there is a supernatural dimension to existence? (20)

10

THE EARLY CHRISTIANS

HOW THEY LIVED

ACTS 2 vv 22–24, 40–47

Fellow-Jews . . . listen to me! (Acts 2 v 14)

ACTS OF THE APOSTLES

The New Testament book called the *Acts of the Apostles* describes what happened to Jesus' followers in the early years after his resurrection. This book was written by the same author as *Luke's Gospel,* probably at some time in the eighties AD.

SUMMARY OF THE TEXT

After Jesus' resurrection, his closest followers, including Peter, had another intensely religious experience.

They felt that Jesus had sent to them the gift of God's Holy Spirit.

The story is told at the beginning of this chapter in the book of *Acts.*

What the gift of the Spirit meant was that the Apostles felt full of energy and confidence, and more: that they had the authority of God Himself to go out to tell everyone about Jesus' life, death and resurrection.

This is what Peter is doing in these verses.

COMMENTARY ON THE TEXT

In this first part of the text, Peter is speaking to a group of fellow Jews, trying to persuade them of Jesus' true identity:

v 22 Jesus of Nazareth was a man whose divine authority was clearly proven to you by all the miracles and wonders which God performed through him.

This was the point which Jesus made himself when he was healing the paralysed man. When the scribes expressed anger at Jesus' forgiving the man's sins, Jesus went on to heal the man as a sign of the authority which had been given to him by God.

v 23 In accordance with his own plan, God had already decided that Jesus would be handed over to you.

There is a strong sense in all the Gospel accounts that the fate of Jesus was all part of God's plan. The *Gospel* writers often find texts from the Old Testament to try and show that His plans about Jesus were even written there. These are called *proof texts*.

The Old Testament Book of *Isaiah* is used a lot to provide proof texts.

(i)   To show that John the Baptist's work as a forerunner of Jesus was foretold in the Bible, Mark uses *Isaiah 40 v 3: A voice cries out, 'Prepare in the wilderness a road for the Lord.'*

(ii) Each year at our carol services we listen to *Isaiah 9 v 6*. These verses, written several hundred years before the time of Jesus, are read to show that his birth was part of God's plan:

> *A child is born to us!*
>
> *A son is given to us!*
>
> *And he will be our ruler,*
>
> *. . . 'Prince of Peace'*

217

(iii) Jesus' followers had to explain why Jesus was not the sort of Messiah the people expected. In *Isaiah 53 v 3* are what have been called the 'servant' verses. Here the prophet talks about a servant of the Lord who has suffered. Jesus' followers saw in these verses a perfect description of exactly what happened to Jesus in the last week of his life.

Isaiah 53 v 3 *We despised him, rejected him; he endured suffering and pain . . .*

This seemed to show that the sad end to Jesus' life had already been predicted by the Old Testament prophet.

Peter in his preaching, therefore, used the Old Testament in this way. *Acts 2 vv 25–28* is taken directly from *Psalm 16 vv 8–11*. To prove his point in *verse 24* that, 'It was impossible that death should hold him a prisoner,' Peter quoted *Psalm 16,* in which one of the verses reads, 'You will not allow your faithful servant to rot in the grave.'

This is a good example of one of Jesus' followers using a proof text from the Old Testament to prove his claim about Jesus.

Peter's words also show what the followers of Jesus quite quickly came to believe about him. The first people whom they tried to persuade to believe in him were Jews like themselves.

vv 42–47 *The way of life of the first believers*

v 42 *. . . sharing in the fellowship meals . . .*

Those who first believed in Jesus would meet together to hear the Apostles repeat what Jesus taught them. When together, they would share bread and pass wine around among themselves. Jesus had told his disciples to do this at his Last Supper with them. So, after his death, whenever his followers met, they would break bread and share wine in that way to remember him. This also bound them together in a special way, as they believed that in this breaking of bread Jesus was actually present with them.

Today that meal is called *Holy Communion* and it still takes place in people's homes as well as in churches.

v 43 *Many miracles and wonders were being done through the apostles, and everyone was filled with awe.*

The Apostles had been given the same power from God as Jesus had. Therefore, they healed the sick and cast out evil spirits in Jesus' name as further proof that Jesus was the Messiah.

For the writer of *Acts* this was evidence that a new age had dawned: the age of God's Kingdom.

v 45 *They would sell their property and possessions, and distribute the money among all, according to what each one needed.*

These actions remind us of Jesus' suggestion to the rich young man that he should sell everything and give the money raised to the poor.

Clearly the text records the actions of some of the first Christians who as a group decided to sell property and share possessions. This means that some of them probably lived together in what we would call a *commune*. Their life together would include regular prayer each day. This is how monks and nuns have lived in their communities throughout the centuries and still do today.

But from the earliest times it would be the exception rather than the rule for Jesus' followers to live in this communal way and for them to give away all that they had.

v 46 *Day after day they met as a group in the Temple . . .*

This is a reminder to us that in these earliest times Jesus' followers remained Jews. They would naturally still observe Jewish religious rules and be happy to meet in the Temple. The verse does go on to say that they had their meals together in their homes. This can mean ordinary daily meals, but it probably also refers to the 'fellowship' meals mentioned above which included the breaking and sharing of bread which would in the end mark them out as starting a religion separate from Judaism.

Questions on the Commentary

1. Copy out this sentence and fill in the missing words:

   The *Acts of the Apostles* was written by .... probably around AD ....

2. What was the aim of Peter's message to his fellow Jews?

3. What is meant by a *proof text*?

4. Give some examples of how proof texts were used in the New Testament, explaining why each of your examples was chosen by the author.

5. Show which proof text Peter uses in this passage and explain how he uses it.

6. What does *fellowship meals* mean in the passage?

7. For the writer of *Acts* what do the miracles and wonders performed by the Apostles show?

8. What is shown by the fact that these earliest believers continued to meet in the Temple?

CONTEMPORARY ISSUES

1. A CARING COMMUNITY

Rene was forty-three when she was told that she had nine months to live. She lived on the second floor of a tower block in the East End of London with her husband and two children aged ten and eight.

The news had been given to her by Sister Agnes and Sister Margaret from St Joseph's Hospice. Hospices offer time with good nurses to answer your questions honestly and to make sure that you are free of pain. They don't give up on you when

220

you can't be cured. In the bad old days you were just put in a corner of a hospital ward and left to earn your painkillers every four hours according to how bad your pain was. That was barbaric!

Now, thank God, hospices like St Joseph's give you all the pain relief you need and they tell you the truth about your illness, just as Agnes and Margaret had told the truth to Rene.

Once she knew, like all mums, Rene's first thoughts were for the children. So she put aside some of her family allowance each week to save up for a surprise holiday in Spain for them when she had gone.

The Sisters helped her remain at home right to the end, apart, that is, from the holiday they arranged for Rene and her family to have in Norfolk three weeks before she died. In her final weeks Rene made a long tape-recording of her thanks to all the neighbours who had been so good to her. She felt that the people round her had really supported her in her trouble. On the tape she thanked them in detail for all the jobs they had taken on for her: the washing, the shopping, the ironing, looking after the kids while she went for her chemotherapy.

Rene also found space on the tape to thank the two Sisters for their daily visits to nurse her and for giving her confidence about what she had to face. Most of all she thanked them for keeping her secret about Spain.

1. How do hospices help the terminally ill?

2. What kind of support did Rene find from her neighbours?

3. Why do you think that those in the hospice movement believe in offering honest answers to patients like Rene?

4. Find out more about your local hospice so that you can prepare a school assembly on hospice care.

2. **THE BOOK IN THE SKY**

Rachael used to get really fed up with her dad smoking. As a coalman he could not have worked harder, carrying bags of coal in all weathers. The bags were really heavy when they were wet as well. Then there was his horse to bed down for the night and to dry off.

'What other pleasures do I 'av?' he would say. 'I don't drink, I don't gamble, I don't go to the races . . . it's all I spend my money on. The rest goes to your mam.'

He was right. In fact, he used to hand his wage packet unopened to mam and she would give him his cigarette money back. That's all he carried around, his money for fags.

'But you'll die dad. Those fags will kill you.'

'Listen, love', he would say, 'up there in heaven, there's the book of life and written in it is my name: Jim Miller. Alongside it is a date. The date for me to pop me clogs. It's there in black and white and there's nothing that you, I, nor anyone else can do owt about. So there!'

1. Do you agree with Jim that it is all decided and the date of everyone's death is fixed?

2. If he is right, what does that mean about our lives?

3. If you believe in astrology, do you have to believe that everything that happens has been planned and we are all following a heavenly script?

THE APOSTLES ARE PERSECUTED

ACTS 5 vv 17–42

SUMMARY OF THE TEXT

Jealousy led the High Priest and the party of local Sadducees to put Peter and the Apostles in prison.

That night they were released by an angel who instructed them to go to the Temple to preach about their new life as followers of Jesus.

When the High Priest discovered what had happened, he had them brought back, without force, before his Council.

When accused of disobeying the High Priests' instructions that they must not teach in the name of Jesus, Peter replied that they had to obey God, not man.

Peter then told them that the God of their ancestors had indeed raised Jesus from the dead to be their leader and Saviour, and to give the Jewish people chance to repent of their sins.

On hearing this, the Council were furious enough to have Peter and the Apostles executed.

However, a Pharisee named Gamaliel advised caution.

He reminded the Council of men whose preaching had come to nothing and they had been forgotten.

Gamaliel offered the wise advice that, if what Peter and the Apostles preached was of man's making, then it too would fade away.

But if it really was from God, nothing the Council decided would prevent the teaching taking hold of the people.

The Council took Gamaliel's advice.

They had the Apostles whipped.

For their part, the Apostles felt happy because God had considered them worthy to suffer.

They continued to preach and to teach in Jesus' name.

COMMENTARY ON THE TEXT

v 19 *. . . but that night an angel of the Lord opened the prison gates.*

The mission of the Apostles to spread the Good News about Jesus was too important to be stopped by being locked up in prison, so they were let out by God's messenger.

v 29 *Peter and the other apostles replied . . .*

This was a very formal court and it provided a backdrop for Peter's preaching of the Gospel to the most important religious leaders in the area.

Peter tried to get the Council to understand that Jesus represented continuity with the past. They were not trying to start a new religion. Jesus was part of the same covenant relationship with God that had existed since Abraham and Moses. But now Jesus represented God's most important saving act for Israel.

The Apostles were witnesses to this truth. Peter said that he and they could do no other than to testify to it. It would be impossible for them not to preach about Jesus and what he meant for the Jewish people.

v 34 *. . . a Pharisee named Gamaliel . . .*

This was a time of many false prophets and Gamaliel mentioned two whose movements came to nothing. If those who claimed to be the Messiah were false, it would soon be obvious and their movements would come to nothing in the same way. But, if what Peter and the others were preaching about Jesus were blessed by God, it was bound to prosper and it could not be put down.

A note on Early Church persecution

The Pharisees were a very strict group of Jewish religious leaders, anxious to protect their religion from the ever-present bad influence of Greek and Roman culture.

They were strong on the detail of the law of Moses and on the writings by scribes who over the years had offered helpful interpretations of that law.

The Sadducees, who for the most part came from wealthy families, were a religious party who cared only about the law of Moses. They did not believe in the resurrection of the dead.

Despite these differences, both Pharisees and Sadducees would have been unhappy about the preaching of Peter and the Apostles.

These earliest followers of Jesus stayed Jews and, like Jesus, they continued to attend the synagogues. For them the teaching of Jesus was the next chapter in their Jewish religion.

This is not how the Pharisees and Sadducees would view them. Just as they had so often been in arguments with Jesus, the earliest Christians were to suffer the same fate.

Jesus predicted that this would happen. [Read again on page 138 what Jesus said to James and John when they asked for the best seats at God's banquet].

Also as time went on, Jesus' followers moved on from just thinking of him as God's Messiah. They thought of him as God's Son and then as God Himself in human form (this belief is known as *incarnation*).

Such a belief would be blasphemy to the Jewish religious leaders. It would seem to be against the idea of God as one. There could be no room in the synagogue for any who thought of Jesus in any sense as God.

For their part, the Romans were very tolerant of other religions and when they conquered a nation, they were very careful to respect the gods of that nation. They first began to persecute Christians after the fire of Rome in AD 64.

The Emperor Nero had made himself sufficiently unpopular as to be seen as the chief suspect. He managed to put the blame on the Christians. And so in Rome people were sentenced to death for being Christians.

The Roman historian Tacitus has provided us with this very horrible account of how these Christians were treated by Nero. Tacitus believed that Christians were criminals but he also believed that Nero went too far . . .

> . . . *an immense multitude* (of Christians) *was convicted, not so much of the crime of arson, as of hatred of the human race.*

> *Mockery of every sort was added to their deaths. Covered with the skins of beasts, they were torn by dogs and perished, or were nailed to crosses, or were doomed to the flames.*

> *These served to illuminate the night when daylight failed. Nero had thrown open his garden for the spectacle and was exhibiting a show in the circus while he mingled with the people in the dress of a charioteer.*

But when the people saw these horrible sights in Nero's garden . . .

> . . . *there arose a feeling of compassion; for it was not, as it seemed, for the public good* (that these people had died) *but to glut one man's cruelty that they were being destroyed.*

Things got worse under the Emperor Domitain (81–96) who had called himself 'Master and God'. He set about testing the loyalty of his people by making them drink a toast to him as a god. This caused problems for Jews and Christians who were persecuted if they were not willing to do this.

Questions on the Commentary

1. Why did the High Priest have Peter and the Apostles put in prison?

2. What was Peter's answer to the High Priest when he was forbidden to teach in the name of Jesus?

3. Explain how Peter and the Apostles were spared a death sentence.

4. Why were the earliest Christians persecuted by the Jewish religious leaders?

5. Why did Nero persecute Christians?

6. How did Nero punish Christians?

7. What effect did this punishment have on the people of Rome?

8. After the time of Nero why were Christians persecuted by Rome?

9. Prepare a talk on

   either   (i)   the difficulties faced by Christians today in China

   or   (ii)   how Christianity survived in the Communist USSR.

Common Entrance Questions

1. (a) Who began to persecute the Apostles in Jerusalem because he was jealous of them? (1)

   (b) What punishment was given to the Apostles following this jealousy? (2)

   (c) What was the message the angel of the Lord gave to the Apostles? (2)

   (d) Describe Peter's reply to the High Priest and Council. (5)

   (e) Explain the meaning of Gamaliel's statement to the Council. (5)

   (f) 'Christians must be prepared to suffer for their faith.' Do you agree? Give reasons to support your answer. (10)

2. (a) Which Apostle said, 'Listen to these words, fellow Israelites! Jesus of Nazareth . . .'? (1)

   (b) How many believers joined the Apostles' group on the day of Pentecost? (2)

   (c) How did the believers spend their time? (2)

   (d) Describe some of the activities in the lives of the early followers of Jesus. (5)

   (e) Explain why the Temple was still used by the early believers in Jesus. (5)

   (f) It is often said that religious belief grows stronger in times of danger and persecution. Discuss this view, using examples to back up your answer. (10)

3. (a) Who put the first Christians into prison? (1)

   (b) How did the Apostles escape from prison? (2)

   (c) Who said: 'We must obey God, not men.'? (2)

   (d) What advice did Gamaliel give to the Council? (5)

   (e) Why did this experience encourage the Apostles in their mission? (5)

   (f) Write about someone in recent history who has been prepared to suffer for his/her beliefs. (10)

4. (a) Who seems to have been the spokesman for the disciples in the weeks immediately after Jesus' death and resurrection? (1)

(b) Where did the early Christians meet one another? (2)

(c) Who arrested the early Christians? (2)

(d) Summarise what the early Christians believed and taught about Jesus. (5)

(e) Explain why these beliefs and teachings often led to their being arrested. (5)

(f) The early Christians sold their property and possessions. Do you think that today our property and possessions are too important to us? Give examples and reasons for your views. (10)

Scholarship Questions

1. Do you think that all Christians should *sell their property and possessions, and distribute the money among all, according to what each one needed?* (Acts 2 v 45) (20)

2. Do you agree with the sentiment 'Charity begins at Home!' (20)

3. To what extent do you think that the events of our lives are pre-determined? (20)

4. Jesus was a faithful Jew and, when he died, his followers continued for a while to attend the synagogue as he had done. Explain why this state of affairs did not last and how a new religion came into being. (20)

COMMON ENTRANCE PAPER – SECTION 3 SAMPLE QUESTIONS

Old Testament Texts

Choose the correct answer.

1. After the flood, God sent a sign to show he would never send another flood to destroy the earth – this sign was

   (a) a dove

   (b) a whirlwind

   (c) a rainbow

   (d) a raven. (1)

2. As a punishment for people beginning to think they were gods, God mixed up their

   (a) race

   (b) colour

   (c) religions

   (d) languages. (1)

3. Isaac and Rebecca had twin sons called Esau and

   (a) Benjamin

   (b) Jacob

   (c) Joseph

   (d) Raphael. (1)

4. Jacob was the son of

   (a) Abraham

   (b) David

   (c) Isaac

   (d) Esau. (1)

5. Joseph's brothers were jealous of him, so they

    (a) killed him

    (b) threw him down a well

    (c) fed him to wild beasts

    (d) put him in a cave. (1)

6. Moses' sister was called

    (a) Rachael

    (b) Miriam

    (c) Jochebed

    (d) Naomi. (1)

7. Moses saw a burning

    (a) fire

    (b) tree

    (c) bush

    (d) forest. (1)

8. Moses' brother was called

    (a) Jacob

    (b) Benjamin

    (c) Aaron

    (d) Rubin. (1)

9. Every Israelite family killed a lamb and splashed its blood on the

    (a) wall

    (b) window

    (c) roof

    (d) doorpost. (1)

10. Joshua had to walk round the city seven times and at the sound of the trumpet the people had to

   (a) charge

   (b) bow down in prayer

   (c) shout

   (d) retreat.   (1)

11. Samson fought against

   (a) the Midianites

   (b) the Philistines

   (c) the Benjaminites

   (d) the Hebrews.   (1)

12. Samson killed

   (a) Midianites

   (b) lions

   (c) locusts

   (d) Philistines.   (1)

13. Ruth was born in the country called

   (a) Philistia

   (b) Samaria

   (c) Moab

   (d) Egypt.   (1)

14. Naomi was the mother-in-law of

   (a) Ruth

   (b) Sarah

   (c) Leah

   (d) Esther.   (1)

15. Ruth's mother-in-law was called

    (a) Naomi

    (b) Orpah

    (c) Esther

    (d) Sarah. (1)

16. David struck Goliath with a

    (a) stone

    (b) sword

    (c) spear

    (d) slap. (1)

17. Goliath was champion of the

    (a) Midianites

    (b) Hittites

    (c) Canaanites

    (d) Philistines. (1)

18. As the price to marry his younger daughter, Saul asked David to kill

    (a) thirty

    (b) one thousand

    (c) two hundred

    (d) forty (1)

    Philistines.

19. King Ahab was married to

    (a) Delilah

    (b) Jezebel

    (c) Ruth

    (d) Sarah.

20. Jezebel had Naboth accused of

    (a) robbery

    (b) murder

    (c) treason

    (d) arson. (1)

21. The great man in Syria who had a skin disease was

    (a) Boaz

    (b) Aaron

    (c) Shunen

    (d) Naaman. (1)

22. As a cure, Elisha asked Naaman to

    (a) climb a holy mountain

    (b) bathe in the Jordan

    (c) eat no unclean food

    (d) pray seven times each day. (1)

23. Jeremiah went to the house of a

    (a) blacksmith

    (b) builder

    (c) potter

    (d) vinedresser (1)

    to watch him work.

24. Daniel was thrown into a pit of

    (a) lions

    (b) snakes

    (c) mud

    (d) wolves. (1)

25. After the death of Nebuchadnezzar, the king of Babylon was

    (a) Jehoram

    (b) Ahab

    (c) Hezekiah

    (d) Belshazzar.   (1)

26. Esther became Queen of

    (a) Egypt

    (b) Israel

    (c) Persia

    (d) Greece.   (1)

27. Esther's father was called

    (a) Haman

    (b) Mordecai

    (c) Samson

    (d) Belshazzar.   (1)

28. Jonah was asked by God to preach to the people of

    (a) Tarshish

    (b) Ninevah

    (c) Persia

    (d) Joppa.

New Testament Texts

29. Mary was visited by an angel called

    (a) Melchior

    (b) Michael

    (c) Gabriel

    (d) Gideon.   (1)

30. Joseph and Mary had to go to Bethlehem because

    (a) it was Joseph's home town

    (b) Jesus was about to be born

    (c) the shepherds were there

    (d) they wanted to escape Herod.   (1)

31. As a boy, Jesus was missing from his parents because

    (a) he had gone to the synagogue

    (b) he was offering a sacrifice in the Temple

    (c) he was listening to teachers in the Temple

    (d) he had stayed too long in prayer.   (1)

32. John the Baptist told people to

    (a) repent

    (b) be like the good Samaritan

    (c) cross the Jordan

    (d) go to church.   (1)

33. Jesus changed water into wine when he attended a wedding in the town of

    (a) Nazareth

    (b) Bethlehem

    (c) Jerusalem

    (d) Cana.   (1)

34. Before he became a disciple of Jesus, Peter was a

    (a) doctor

    (b) tax-collector

    (c) soldier

    (d) fisherman.   (1)

35. Simon, James and John were

    (a) fishermen

    (b) carpenters

    (c) farmers

    (d) shepherds.   (1)

36. Jesus taught his followers to pray that his

    (a) Kingdom

    (b) Messiahship

    (c) Life

    (d) Death

    might come.   (1)

37. John was beheaded because he

    (a) was a follower of Jesus

    (b) broke God's law

    (c) had argued with Herod

    (d) angered Pontius Pilate.   (1)

38. Jesus healed the Roman officer's servant because of the officer's

    (a) rank

    (b) faith

    (c) donations to the synagogue

    (d) power.   (1)

39. Jesus fed a large crowd with

    (a) locusts

    (b) wild honey

    (c) manna

    (d) fish and bread. (1)

40. Mary and Martha had a brother called

    (a) John

    (b) Levi

    (c) Lazarus

    (d) Zacharius. (1)

41. Jesus was betrayed by

    (a) Peter

    (b) Thomas

    (c) Barabbas

    (d) Judas. (1)

42. Jesus was tried by

    (a) Herodias

    (b) Pharoah

    (c) Xerxes

    (d) Pontius Pilate. (1)

43. Jesus was crucified at a place called

    (a) Golgotha

    (b) Gethsemane

    (c) Gilgal

    (d) Gotham. (1)

44. Jesus was arrested in the garden of

    (a) Gethsemane

    (b) Golgotha

    (c) Eden

    (d) Joseph of Aramathea.   (1)

45. Jesus ate a last supper with his disciples to keep the feast of

    (a) Passover

    (b) Purim

    (c) Tabernacles

    (d) Pentecost.   (1)

46. At the moment Jesus died, the

    (a) altar

    (b) Bible

    (c) curtain

    (d) carpet

    in the Temple was cut in two.

47. On the day of Pentecost, when the disciples were together, there was a sudden rush of

    (a) water

    (b) wind

    (c) people

    (d) sound.   (1)

48. Stephen was killed by

    (a) arrows

    (b) a sword

    (c) hanging

    (d) stones.   (1)

49. Paul was converted to Christianity when he was on the road to

    (a) Jerusalem

    (b) Damascus

    (c) Caesarea Philippi

    (d) Samaria. (1)

50. Paul said that there was faith hope and

    (a) courage

    (b) love

    (c) despair

    (d) discipleship. (1)

Answer the following in one or two full sentences (2 marks each).

51. How did Jacob fool his father Isaac into giving him the blessing instead of his brother Esau?

52. What did Joshua order his people to do on the seventh day of the siege of Jericho?

53. What did Elisha tell Naaman the Syrian to do to get rid of his incurable skin disease?

54. What was the reaction of the people of Jerusalem when Jeremiah told them to give in to the Babylonians?

55. What news did the angel bring to Zechariah the priest in Jerusalem?

56. Why did God destroy the Tower of Babel?

57. What did Jacob do to fool his father?

58. Why was the baker unhappy with the news which Joseph gave him?

59. What was so special about Ruth?

60. Why did Moses kill an Egyptian?

61. How did Rahab help two of Joshua's men?

62. What secret about Samson's strength did Delilah eventually discover?

63. Why did God ask Jonah to go to Ninevah?

64. What news did Gabriel bring to Mary?

65. Why did Joseph and Mary travel to Bethlehem?

66. Which gifts did the Wise Men bring to the baby Jesus?

67. When Jesus was twelve, where was he when he was lost from his parents?

68. What was John's message to those who came to be baptised by him?

69. What did Jesus say to Peter and Andrew when he first met them and they had hauled a huge catch of fish ashore?

70. What did Jesus do at the wedding at Cana in Galilee?

71. According to a parable told by Jesus, how did the merchant gain a beautiful pearl?

72. What other kind of bread did Jesus talk about after feeding five thousand people?

73. Why was Martha annoyed with her sister Mary?

74. Why was John the Baptist put in prison by King Herod?

75. Why was John the Baptist executed?

76. How did Jesus enter Jerusalem for his last Passover festival?

77. What was written on the notice which was fixed to Jesus' cross?

78. What was the reaction of Thomas when he heard that Jesus had appeared to the disciples after his death?

79. What happened to the disciples on the day of Pentecost?

Write a short paragraph to answer the following questions (5 marks).

80. What happened to Paul as he was on the road to Damascus?

81. Describe how Jacob managed to gain the blessing from his father.

82. Describe what happened to Joseph while he was in prison in Egypt.

83. Briefly describe the events of the first Passover at the time of Moses.

84. Describe what happened when Moses saw a burning bush.

85. Describe how Ahab managed to take possession of a vineyard.

86. Describe how a Syrian army commander was healed of a skin disease.

87. Describe how Joshua conquered Jericho.

88. Describe who visited Jesus when he was born and explain the importance of these particular visitors.

89. Retell the parable Jesus told about the wheat and the weeds.

90. Describe how Jesus fed five thousand people.

91. Describe what Jesus said to his disciples during the last supper.

92. Outline very briefly the important events up to the end of supper on the day before Jesus died.

93. Describe the events which took place on the Sunday morning after Jesus was crucified.

94. Describe how Jesus was tried and sentenced to death.

95. Describe what happened when Jesus appeared on the road to Emmaus.

96. Describe what happened when Philip met a man from Ethiopia.